T0149630

The Contemporary Music Harmony Book

Expand your knowledge and understanding of contemporary Music Harmony

By:

Kiki Sanchez

El Libro de Armonía Contemporánea

Amplíe sus conocimientos y comprensión de la armonía contemporánea

Por:

Kiki Sanchez

authorHOUSE®

AuthorHouse™
1663 Liberty Drive
Bloomington, IN 47403
www.authorhouse.com
Phone: 1 (800) 839-8640

Published by AuthorHouse 08/07/2018

ISBN: 978-1-5462-5485-0 (sc)
ISBN: 978-1-5462-5484-3 (e)

Print information available on the last page.

Any people depicted in stock imagery provided by Getty Images are models, and such images are being used for illustrative purposes only.
Certain stock imagery © Getty Images.

This book is printed on acid-free paper.

The purpose of this book is to share Sanchez's years of studying of traditional and contemporary music harmony with other musicians and students. Sanchez had the wonderful idea to write this book that would expose and teach the most important elements of harmony such as Major, Minor, Dominant 7 (#9, #11, and 13), Slash, Tritone Sub, and many others harmony elements.

Sanchez' vision is to expand your musical abilities and for you to have a better understanding of music harmony functions. This information will help on your piano abilities and enrich your musical knowledge as a producer, arranger, and educator.

El propósito de este libro es de compartir los años de estudio de Sanchez relacionados a la armonía tradicional y contemporánea con otros músicos y estudiantes. Sanchez tuvo la maravillosa idea de escribir este libro que expone y enseña los más importantes elementos de la armonía, tales como acordes Mayores, Menores, Dominantes 7 (#9, #11 y 13), Slash, Tritone Sub y muchos más elementos de la armonía.

La visión de Sanchez es expandir tus habilidades musicales y para que tengas una mejor comprensión de cómo funciona la armonía en la música. Esta información ayudará en tus habilidades de piano y enriquecerá tus conocimientos musicales como productor, arreglista y educador.

About the Author

The extraordinarily Peruvian producer, composer, arranger, educator, and pianist Luis Enrique "Kiki" Sanchez can capture the hearts of many through his variations of skillful and unique style that have filled the airwaves with a distinctive blend of soulful jazz, tropical, and Afro-Peruvian fusion. This gifted musician was born and raised in Lima, Peru where he studied piano with Coco Macedo and Edermi Chavez and started playing professionally at the age of 11. He became a well-rounded musician by playing with his father's band "Orquesta Majestic" doing corporate venues in Lima. Later he moved to Miami, FL where he has worked with several Jazz and Latin Jazz Artists. He continued to expand his knowledge and education at the Florida Atlantic University where Sanchez earned a Master Degree in Music Composition.

His musical journey has led Sanchez to release two Latin Jazz albums:

- **"Dreams"** (Diola Entertainment 2007)

- **"Two Worlds"** (Diola Entertainment 2011) featuring Grammy Award winner Susana Baca.

Sanchez's vision is to reach several audiences and expand his musical abilities by releasing projects from different genders.

- **"In a Quiet and Healing Mood"** (Estreno Digital 2015) Music Meditation Album, this is Sanchez' most important project because it achieves the real purpose of music which is to bring peace, energy, love and understanding.

- **"Kiki Sanchez Salsa Project"** Soneros del Peru (Diola Entertainment 2016)

- **"Too Many Notes"** his latest single, this is the first track of the Kiki Sanchez Jazz Big Band Project released on May, 2016

Kiki has been nominated for the Grammys in several projects such as:

- "Blown Away" from Frankie Marcus featuring Arturo Sandoval where Sanchez programmed Keyboards and played piano. (Universal Music)

- "La Onda Latina", Frankie Marcus and Clouds was nominated for Best Traditional Tropical Album where Kiki arranged, programmed, and recorded piano. (Estreno Digital)
- "Back to Basic" from Edwin Bonilla (Gloria Estefan's percussionist) where Kiki composed, arranged and recorded the piano on the track title "Descarga Para El Bailador" (Sonic Project Records)
- Kiki has collaborated with Grammy-winning producer, Glen Kolotkin in numerous projects as well. Nowadays Kiki Sanchez is a voting member of the Grammy Awards Academy.

As an educator, Sanchez has also released an Educational DVD titled **"The Real Latin Piano and Introduction to Afro-Peruvian Rhythms"** (2009) published by ADG Productions and the book **"The Real Latin Piano Book"** published in 2012 by ADG Productions.

Kiki has been doing music clinics and workshops in the States and overseas. He is currently a Music professor at Miami Dade College and also he has been teaching music technology courses at Palm Beach Atlantic University.

Sanchez is very active as an artist, producer arranger, educator, and pianist. He performed at the inauguration of the Larry Rosen "Jazz Roots" at the Arsht Center in Miami, FL. He also has been the music director of several musical theaters in South Florida.

Kiki also has performed in several Jazz Festivals such as Montreux, St. Lucia, Grenada, Ohio Jazz and Rib and others. He also has been the music director for "Noches Tropicales" Jazz series at Miami Dade County Auditorium.

Recently, Sanchez has been performing locally and overseas, during the summer of 2015, he performed at the SFJAZZ Center in San Francisco, CA, Instituto Cervantes in New York, Kirchner Cultural Center in Buenos Aires, Argentina, and several other places.

Kiki is also the Music Outreach Director of Beauliere Academy of Music in Haiti, where he goes every summer to provide music education.

Kiki was the Director of Music Department at Hurst Chapel A.M.E Church in Riviera Beach, Florida and currently, he is the Director of Music Department at Ebenezer United Methodist Church located in Miami, Florida.

In the near future Kiki plans to release two Latin Jazz singles titled **"Sanchez's Blues"** and **"It is a Peruvian Thing"** by Diola Entertainment. Additionally, he will also release two other Gospel singles **"I Praise You Lord"** and **"I Want to Give You My Best"**.

Finally, Sanchez is so excited about his 501C3 Non-Profit Organization "PWW (Place for Praise and Worship)" where the mission is to help and provide music education to kids from less fortunate families and communities. One of Sanchez' dreams is to make a difference through Arts/Music education and to expose its benefits through "PWW" journey.

Kiki Sanchez has been honored to receive the CASIO, Japan endorsement for Latin America.

Luis Enrique "Kiki" Sanchez M.A.

www.kikisanchez.com

www.facebook.com/KikiSanchezMusic

http://twitter.com/KikiSanchez1

Sobre el Autor

El extraordinariamente peruano productor, compositor, arreglista, educador y pianista Luis Enrique "Kiki" Sánchez puede capturar los corazones de muchos a través de sus variaciones de estilo hábil y único que han llenado las ondas con una mezcla distintiva de jazz soul, tropical y afro- Fusión peruana. Este talentoso músico nació y creció en Lima, Perú, donde estudió piano con Coco Macedo y Edermi Chávez y empezó a tocar profesionalmente a la edad de 11 años. Se convirtió en un músico bien formado tocando con la banda de su padre "Orquesta Majestic" haciendo eventos corporativos en Lima. Posteriormente se trasladó a Miami, FL, donde trabajó con varios artistas de Jazz Latinos. Él continuó ampliando sus conocimientos y educación en la Florida Atlantic University donde Sánchez obtuvo su Maestría en Composición Musical.

Su viaje musical ha llevado a Sánchez a lanzar dos álbumes de jazz latino:

- **"Dreams" "Sueños"** (Diola Entertainment 2007)
- **"Two Worlds" "Dos Mundos"** (Diola Entertainment 2011) con la ganadora del premio Grammy Susana Baca.

La visión de Sánchez es llegar a varios públicos y expandir sus habilidades musicales lanzando proyectos de diferentes géneros como:

- **"In a Quiet and Healing Mood" "En un Ambiente Tranquilo y Curativo"** (Estreno Digital 2015) un álbum de Meditación musical, este es el álbum más importante de Sanchez porque logra el verdadero propósito de la música que es traer paz, energía, amor y comprensión.
- **"Kiki Sanchez Salsa Project"** Soneros del Perú (Diola Entertainment 2016)
- **"Too Many Notes",** es su más reciente sencillo, esta es la primera canción del Kiki Sanchez Jazz Big Band Project que fue lanzado en Mayo del 2016.

Kiki ha sido nominado a los Premios de la Academia Grammy en varios proyectos como:

- "Blown Away" de Frankie Marcus con Arturo Sandoval donde Sánchez programó los teclados y tocó el piano (Universal Music).
- "La Onda Latina", Frankie Marcus y Clouds, que fue nominado al Mejor Álbum Tropical Tradicional donde Kiki arregló, programó y grabó el piano (Estreno Digital).
- "Back to Basic" de Edwin Bonilla (percusionista de Gloria Estefan) donde Kiki compuso, arregló y grabó el piano en el tema "Descarga Para El Bailador" (Sonic Project Records).

Kiki ha colaborado con el ganador del Grammy, Glen Kolotkin en numerosos proyectos. Actualmente Kiki Sánchez es miembro votante de la Academia de los Premios Grammy.

Como educador, Sánchez también ha lanzado un DVD educativo **titulado "El Verdadero piano Latino y la Introducción a los Ritmos Afroperuanos"** (2009) publicado por ADG Productions y el libro **"The Real Latin Piano Book"** publicado en 2012 por ADG Productions.

Kiki ha estado haciendo clínicas de música y talleres en los Estados Unidos y en el extranjero. Actualmente es profesor de música en el Miami Dade College y también ha estado enseñando cursos de tecnología musical en Palm Beach Atlantic University.

Sánchez es muy activo como artista, arreglista productor, educador y pianista. Se presentó en la inauguración de Larry Rosen "Jazz Roots" en el Arsht Center en Miami, FL. También ha sido el director musical de varias obras musicales en el sur de la Florida.

Kiki también ha tocado en varios Festivales de Jazz como: Montreal, Santa Lucía, Granada, Ohio Jazz y Rib y otros. También ha sido director musical de la serie Jazz de "Noches Tropicales" en el Miami Dade County Auditórium.

Recientemente, Sánchez ha estado actuando localmente y en el extranjero, durante el verano de 2015, actuó en el SFJAZZ Center en San Francisco, CA, el Instituto Cervantes en Nueva York, el Centro Cultural Kirchner en Buenos Aires, Argentina y muchos otros lugares.

Kiki es también el Director de Extensión Musical de la Academia de Música de Beauliere en Haití, donde va cada verano para ofrecer educación musical.

Kiki fue Director de Departamento de Música en la Iglesia de Hurst Chapel A.M.E en Riviera Beach, Florida y actualmente es el Director de Departamento de Música de la Iglesia Metodista Ebenezer en Miami, FL.

En un futuro próximo, Kiki planea lanzar dos sencillos de jazz latino titulados "Blues de Sánchez" y "Es una cosa Peruana" de Diola Entertainment. Además, también lanzará otros dos sencillos en el género de música Góspel, "Te alabo Señor" y "Quiero darte lo mejor".

Por último, Sánchez está muy emocionado con su organización sin fines de lucro 501C3 "PWW (Lugar de Alabanza y Culto)", donde la misión es ayudar y proveer educación musical a niños de familias y comunidades menos afortunadas. Uno de los sueños de Sánchez es hacer una diferencia a través de la educación de Artes/Música.

Kiki Sánchez se ha honrado de recibir el respaldo de CASIO de Japón para América Latina.

Luis Enrique "Kiki" Sanchez M.A.

www.kikisanchez.com

www.facebook.com/KikiSanchezMusic

http://twitter.com/KikiSanchez1

Table of Contents

*To obtain a free copy of the Midi files for this book, please contact us at info@kikisanchez.com.

*Para obtener una copia gratuita de los archivos Midi de este libro, póngase en contacto con nosotros en info@kikisanchez.com.

The Major Scale/ La Escala Mayor

- A **Major scale** constructed by seven pitches.

- Una **Escala Mayor** está construida por siete notas.

- This is the Major scale whole & half step construction: W W H -W W W H

- La construcción de una escala Mayor es W (Tono) & H (Semitono)

✓ For Example/ Por Ejemplo: W W H - W W W H

Chords/ Acordes

- A **Major Chord** construction is: Root, 3rd & 5th

- La construcción de un **Acorde Mayor** triada en estado fundamental es: Raíz, 3ra & 5ta

1. Root position, root is on the bottom/ Estado fundamental es cuando la raíz esta debajo.

2. First invertion, 3rd is on the bottom/ Primera inversion es cuando la 3ra esta debajo.

3. Second invertion, 5th is on the bottom/ Segunda inversion es cuando la 5ta esta debajo.

- A **Minor Chord** constructions is: Root, minor 3rd & 5th

- La construcción un **Acorde Menor** es raíz, 3ra bemol & 5ta

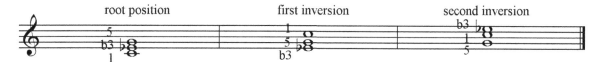

1. Root position, root is on the bottom/ Estado fundamental es cuando la raíz esta debajo.

2. First invertion, b3rd is on the bottom/ Primera inversion es cuando la 3ra bemol esta debajo.

3. Second invertion, 5th is on the bottom/ Segunda inversion es cuando la 5ta esta debajo.

- A **Diminished Chord** construction is root, minor 3rd & b5th

- La construcción del **Acorde Disminuido** es raíz, 3ra menor & 5ta bemol.

- A **Sus4 Chord** construction is root, 4th & 5th.

✓ In Most the cases, the Sus4 Chord resolve to a Mayor chord.

- La construcción del **Acorde Sus/Suspendido** es raíz, 4ta & 5ta.

✓ En muchos casos el acorde Sus4 resuelve a un acorde Mayor.

✓ Here is an example of a Sus4 chord on First and Second inversion:

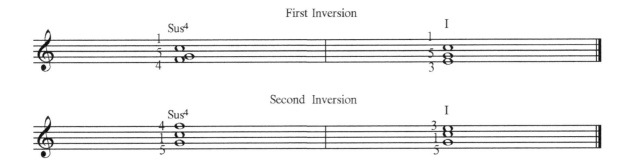

- **C (#5), C+, C+5, Caug or C Augmented** chord construction is root, 3rd & #5.

- La construcción del **Acorde C (#5), C+, C +5, Caug o C Aumentado** es raíz, 3ra & #5.

- A **Sixth Mayor Chord** construction is root, 3rd & 6th

- La construcción del **Acorde de Sexta Mayor** es raíz, 3ra & 6ta.

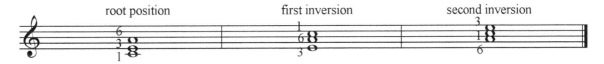

- A **Sixth Minor Chord** constructions is root, minor 3rd & 6th

- La construcción de un **Acorde de Sexta Menor** es raíz, 3ra bemol & 6ta.

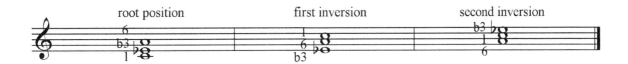

- A **Flat Sixth Minor Chord** constructions is root, minor 3rd & b6th

- La construcción de un **Acorde de Sexta Bemol Menor** es raíz, 3ra bemol & 6ta.

- A **Dominant 7th** Chord construction is root, 3rd, 5th & b7th

- La construcción del **Acorde 7ma Dominante** es raíz, 3ra, 5ta & b7ma.

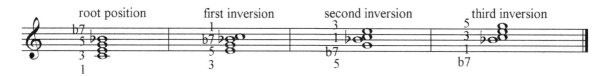

✓ A Dominant 7th chord always will be the 5th of I or i/ El acorde Dominante siempre va a hacer la Quinta de I o i. For Example/ Por Ejemplo:

✓ Here we have some examples of Dominant 7th chord voicing in solo & ensemble Piano concepts.

✓ Aquí tenemos algunos ejemplos de cómo armonizar un acorde Dominante 7 en concepto de Piano Solo & Ensamble.

✓ On a **Solo concept**, the Piano is covering all the harmony parts.

- ✓ En **concepto de Solo** el Piano es responsable de cubrir todos los movimientos armónicos.

- ✓ On an **Ensemble concept**, there is a rhythm section where the Bass or Electric Bass is playing the chord roots.

- ✓ En **concepto de ensamble** es cuando hay una sesión rítmica donde el Bajo o Bajo Electric ova tocando la tónica de los acordes.

- ✓ Examples of Dominant 7th chord on Solo Piano voicing concept/ Ejemplos de un acorde Dominante 7 en concepto de Piano Solo Voicing:

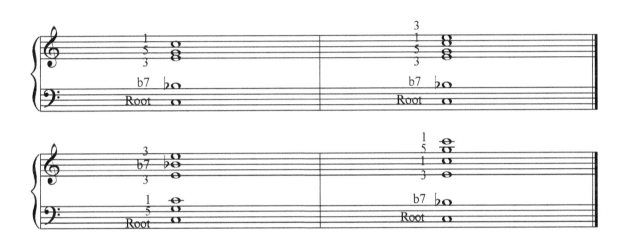

- ✓ Examples of Dominant 7th chord on Ensemble voicing concept/ Ejemplos de un acorde Dominante 7 en concepto de Ensamble voicing:

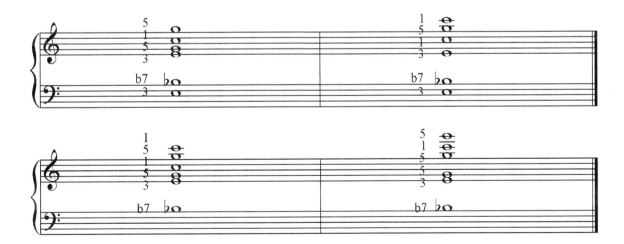

- A **Major 7th chord** construction is root, 3rd, 5th & 7th

- La construcción de un **Acorde de 7ma Mayor** es raíz, 3ra, 5ta & 7ma.

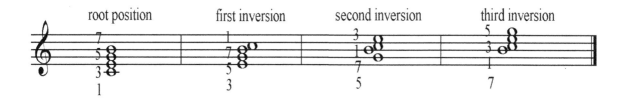

1. Root position, root is on the bottom/ Estado fundamental es cuando la raíz esta debajo.

2. First inversion, 3rd is on the bottom/ Primera inversion es cuando la 3ra esta debajo.

3. Second inversion, 5th is on the bottom/ Segunda inversion es cuando la 5ta esta debajo.

4. Third inversion, 7th in on the bottom/ Tercera inversion es cuando la 7ma esta debajo.

- ✓ Examples of Major 7th chord on Solo Piano voicing concept/ Ejemplos de un acorde Mayor 7 en concepto de Piano Solo Voicing:

✓ Examples of Major 7th chord on Ensemble voicing concept/ Ejemplos de un acorde Mayor 7 en concepto de Ensamble voicing:

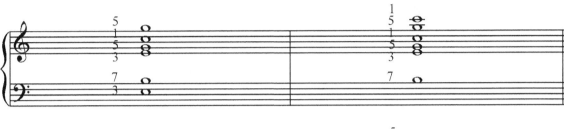

Major Chords & Extensions/ Acordes Mayores & Extensiones

✓ In the next examples, we will learn all the Major chord extensions.

✓ En los próximos ejemplos vamos a aprender todas las extensiones de un acorde Mayor.

- A **Major 9th** chord construction is root, 3rd, 5th, 7th & 9th

- La construcción de un acorde **9na Mayor** es raíz, 3ra, 5ta, 7ma & 9na.

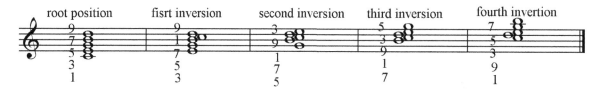

✓ Examples of Major 9th chord on Solo Piano voicing concept/ Ejemplos de un acorde Mayor 9 en concepto de Piano Solo Voicing:

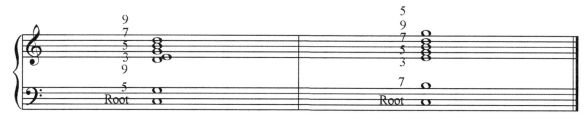

✓ Examples of Major 9th chord on Ensemble voicing concept/ Ejemplos de un acorde Mayor 9 en concepto de Ensamble voicing:

- A **Major #11th** chord construction is root, 3rd, 5th, 7th, 9th & #11th

- La construcción de un acorde **Mayor #11** es raíz, 3ra, 5ta, 7ma, 9na & #11na.

✓ Examples of Major #11th chord on Solo Piano voicing concept/ Ejemplos de un acorde Mayor #11 en concepto de Piano Solo Voicing:

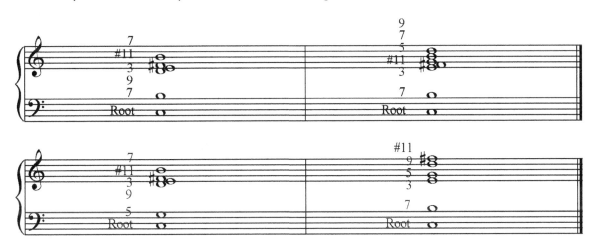

✓ Examples of Major #11ᵗʰ chord on Ensemble voicing concept/ Ejemplos de un acorde Mayor #11 en concepto de Ensamble voicing:

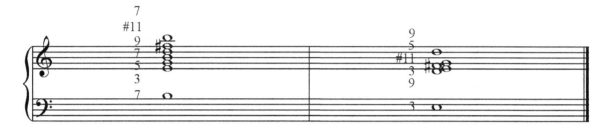

- A **Major 13** chord construction is root, 3ʳᵈ, 5ᵗʰ, 7ᵗʰ, 9ᵗʰ, #11ᵗʰ & 13ᵗʰ

- La construcción de un acorde **Mayor 13na** es raíz, 3ra, 5ta, 7ma, 9na, #11na & 13na.

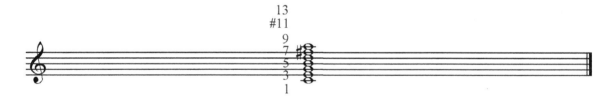

✓ Examples of Major 13ᵗʰ chord on Solo Piano voicing concept/ Ejemplos de un acorde Mayor 13 en concepto de Piano Solo Voicing:

10

✓ Examples of Major 13th chord on Ensemble voicing concept/ Ejemplos de un acorde Mayor 13 en concepto de Ensamble voicing:

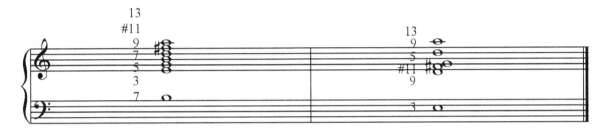

- A **Dominant 7 (9)** chord construction is root, 3rd, 5th, b7th & 9th

✓ There are three types of this kind of chord 9, b9 & #9th

- La construcción del acorde **Dominante 7 (9)** es raíz, 3ra, 5ta, b7ma & 9na.

✓ Existen tres tipos de este acorde 9, b9 & #9.

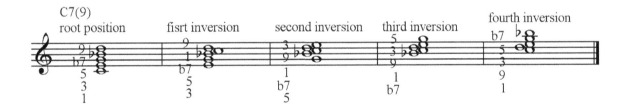

✓ Examples of Dominant 7 (9) chord on Solo Piano voicing concept/ Ejemplos de un acorde Dominante 7 (9) en concepto de Piano Solo Voicing:

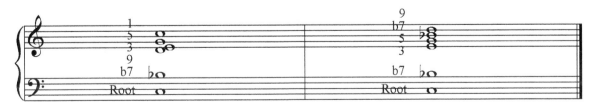

- ✓ Examples of Dominant 7 (9) chord on Ensemble voicing concept/ Ejemplos de un acorde Dominante 7 (9) en concepto de Ensamble voicing:

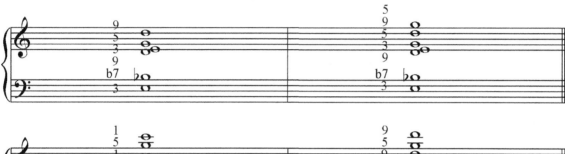

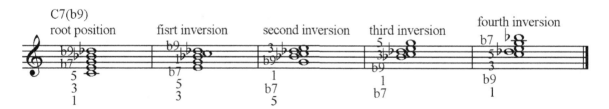

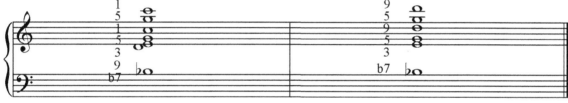

- ✓ Examples of Dominant 7 (b9) chord on Solo Piano voicing concept/ Ejemplos de un acorde Dominante 7 (b9) en concepto de Piano Solo Voicing:

✓ Examples of Dominant 7 (b9) chord on Ensemble voicing concept/ Ejemplos de un acorde Dominante 7 (b9) en concepto de Ensamble Voicing:

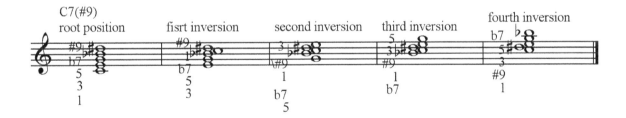

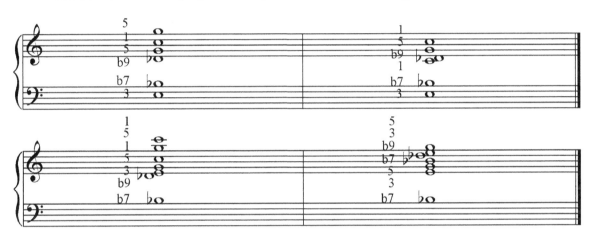

✓ Examples of Dominant 7 (#9) chord on Solo Piano voicing concept/ Ejemplos de un acorde Dominante 7 (#9) en concepto de Piano Solo Voicing:

- ✓ Examples of Dominant 7 (#9) chord on Ensemble voicing concept/ Ejemplos de un acorde Dominante 7 (#9) en concepto de Ensamble voicing:

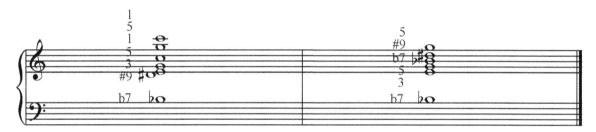

Dominant 7 (9) combinations/Combinaciones de un acorde Dominante 7 (9)

- ✓ In the following examples, we will learn how to combine simultaneously 9, b9 & #9 on a Dominant 7th chord.

- ✓ En los siguientes ejemplos, vamos a aprender como combinar simultáneamente 9, b9 & #9 en un acorde dominante.

- ✓ Examples of Dominant 7 (9, b9 & #9) chord combinations on Solo Piano voicing concept/ Ejemplos de cómo combinar un acorde Dominante 7 (9, b9 & #9) en concepto de Piano Solo Voicing:

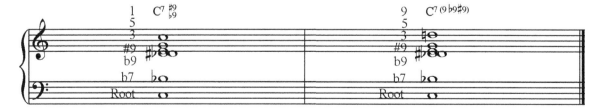

✓ Examples of Dominant 7 (9, b9 & #9) chord combinations on ensemble voicing concept/ Ejemplos de cómo combinar un acorde Dominante 7 (9, b9 & #9) en concepto de Ensemble Voicing:

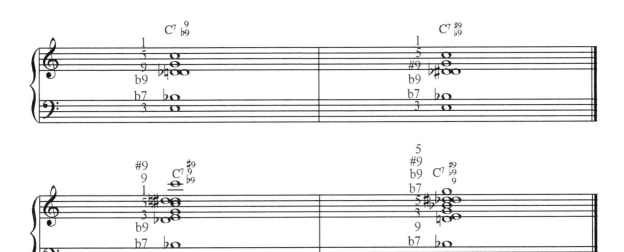

- A **Dominant 7 (9, #11)** chord construction is root, 3rd, 5th, b7th, 9th & #11th

- La construcción del acorde **Dominante 7 (9, #11)** es raíz, 3ra, 5ta, b7ma, 9na & #11na.

✓ Examples of Dominant 7 (9, #11) chord on Solo Piano voicing concept/ Ejemplos de un acorde Dominante 7 (9, #11) en concepto de Piano Solo Voicing:

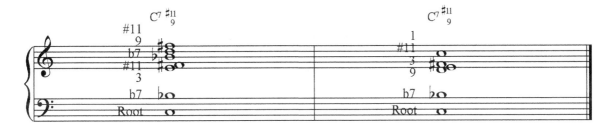

15

✓ Examples of Dominant 7 (9, #11) chord on Ensemble voicing concept/ Ejemplos de un acorde Dominante 7 (9, #11) en concepto de Ensamble Voicing:

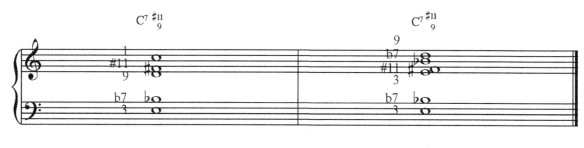

- A **Dominant 7 (b9, #11)** chord construction is root, 3rd, 5th, b7th, b9th & #11th

- La construcción del acorde **Dominante 7 (b9, #11)** es raíz, 3ra, 5ta, b7ma, b9na & #11na.

✓ Examples of Dominant 7 (b9, #11) chord on Solo Piano concept/ Ejemplos de un acorde Dominante 7 (b9, #11) en concepto de Piano Solo Voicing:

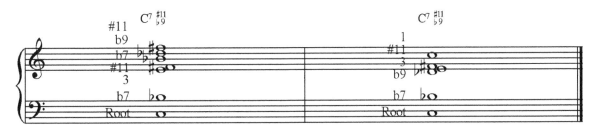

✓ Examples of Dominant 7 (b9, #11) on Ensemble voicing concept/ Ejemplos de un acorde Dominante 7 (b9, #11) en concepto de Ensamble voicing:

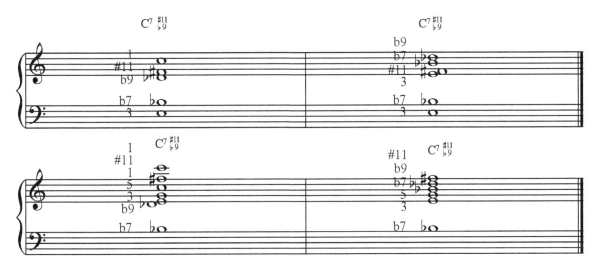

- A **Dominant 7 (#9, #11)** chord construction is root, 3rd, 5th, b7th, #9th & #11th

- La construcción del acorde **Dominante 7 (#9, #11)** es raíz, 3ra, 5ta, b7ma, #9na & #11na.

✓ Examples of Dominant 7 (#9, #11) chord on Solo Piano concept/ Ejemplos de un acorde Dominante 7 (#9, #11) en concepto de Piano Solo Voicing:

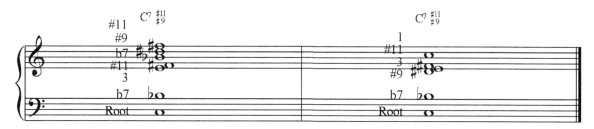

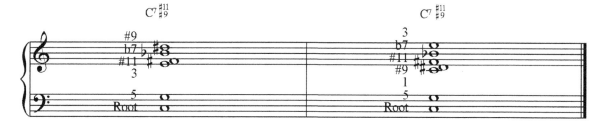

✓ Examples of Dominant 7 (b9, #11) on Ensemble voicing concept/ Ejemplos de un acorde Dominante 7 (b9, #11) en concepto de Ensamble voicing:

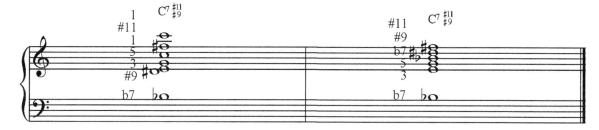

- A **Dominant 7 (13)** chord construction is root, 3rd, 5th, b7th & 13th

- La construcción del acorde **Dominante 7 (13)** es raíz, 3ra, 5ta, b7ma & 13na.

✓ Examples of Dominant 7 (13) chord on Solo Piano concept/ Ejemplos de un acorde Dominante 7 (13) en concepto de Piano Solo Voicing:

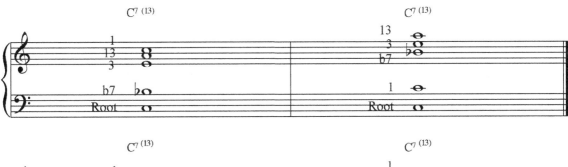

✓ Examples of Dominant 7 (13) on Ensemble voicing concept/ Ejemplos de un acorde Dominante 7 (13) en concepto de Ensamble Voicing:

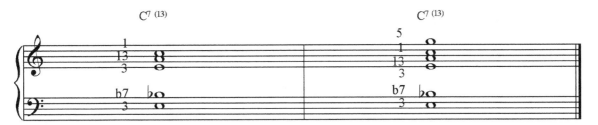

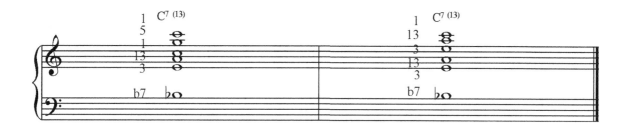

- A **Dominant 7 13 (9, #11)** chord construction is root, 3rd, 5th, b7th, 9th, #11th & 13th

- La construcción del acorde **Dominante 7 13 (9, #11)** es raíz, 3ra, 5ta, b7ma, 9na, #11na & 13na.

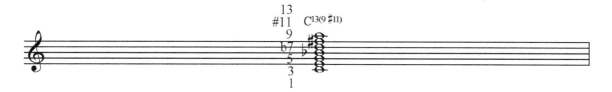

✓ Examples of Dominant 7 13 (9, #11) chord on Solo Piano concept/ Ejemplos de un acorde Dominante 7 13 (9, #11) en concepto de Piano Solo Voicing:

✓ Examples of Dominant 7 13 (9, #11) on Ensemble voicing concept/ Ejemplos de un acorde Dominante 7 13 (9, #11) en concepto de Ensamble Voicing:

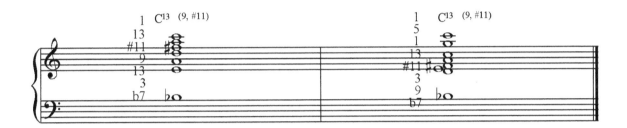

- A **Dominant 7 13 (b9, #11)** chord construction is root, 3rd, 5th, b7th, b9th, #11th & 13th

- La construcción del acorde **Dominante 7 13 (b9, #11)** es raíz, 3ra, 5ta, b7ma, b9na, #11na & 13na.

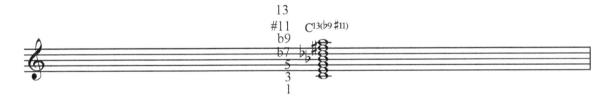

✓ Examples of Dominant 7 13 (b9, #11) chord on Solo Piano concept/ Ejemplos de un acorde Dominante 7 13 (b9, #11) en concepto de Piano Solo Voicing:

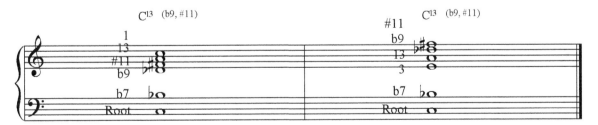

21

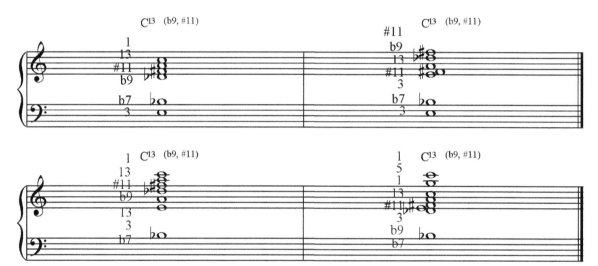

✓ Examples of Dominant 7 13 (b9, #11) on Ensemble voicing concept/ Ejemplos de un acorde Dominante 7 13 (b9, #11) en concepto de Ensamble Voicing:

- A **Dominant 7 13 (#9, #11)** chord construction is root, 3rd, 5th, b7th, #9th, #11th &13th

- La construcción del acorde **Dominante 7 13 (#9, #11)** es raíz, 3ra, 5ta, b7ma, #9na, #11na & 13na.

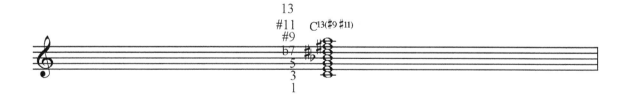

- Examples of Dominant 7 13 (#9, #11) chord on Solo Piano concept/ Ejemplos de un acorde Dominante 7 13 (#9, #11) en concepto de Piano Solo Voicing:

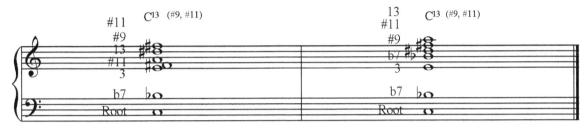

- Examples of Dominant 7 13 (#9, #11) on Ensemble voicing concept/ Ejemplos de un acorde Dominante 7 13 (#9, #11) en concepto de Ensamble Voicing:

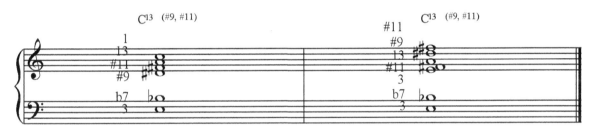

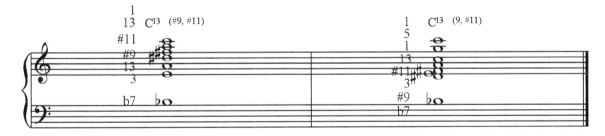

- A **Dominant 7 b13 (9, #11)** chord construction is root, 3rd, 5th, b7th, 9th, #11th & b13th

- La construcción del acorde **Dominante 7 b13 (9, #11)** es raíz, 3ra, 5ta, b7ma, 9na, #11na & b13na

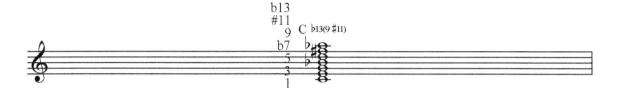

- ✓ Examples of Dominant 7 b13 (9, #11) chord on Solo Piano concept/ Ejemplos de un acorde Dominante 7 b13 (9, #11) en concepto de Piano Solo Voicing:

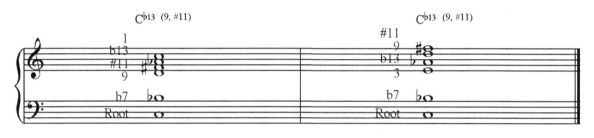

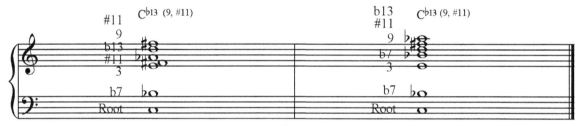

- ✓ Examples of Dominant 7 b13 (9, #11) on Ensemble voicing concept/ Ejemplos de un acorde Dominante 7 b13 (9, #11) en concepto de Ensamble Voicing:

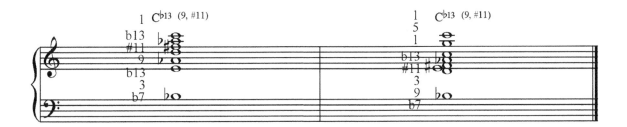

- A **Dominant 7 b13 (b9, #11)** chord construction is root, 3rd, 5th, b7th, b9th, #11th & b13th

- La construcción del acorde **Dominante 7 b13 (b9, #11)** es raíz, 3ra, 5ta, b7ma, b9na, #11na & b13na.

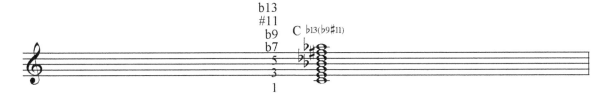

✓ Examples of Dominant 7 b13 (b9, #11) chord on Solo Piano concept/ Ejemplos de un acorde Dominante 7 b13 (b9, #11) en concepto de Piano Solo Voicing:

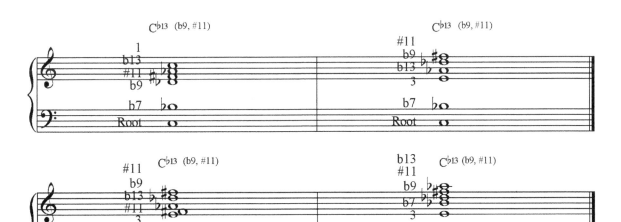

✓ Examples of Dominant 7 b13 (b9, #11) on Ensemble voicing concept/ Ejemplos de un acorde Dominante b13 (b9, #11) en concepto de Ensamble Voicing:

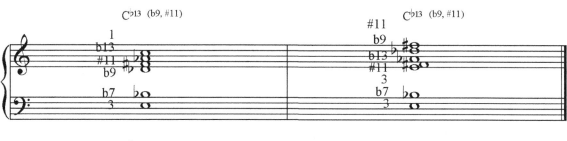

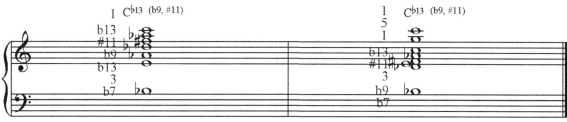

- A **Dominant 7 b13 (#9, #11)** chord construction is root, 3rd, 5th, b7th, #9th, #11th & b13th

- La construcción del acorde **Dominante 7 b13 (#9, #11)** es raíz, 3ra, 5ta, b7ma, #9na, #11na & b13na.

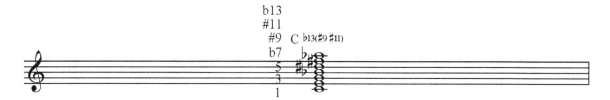

✓ Examples of Dominant 7 b13 (#9, #11) chord on Solo Piano concept/ Ejemplos de un acorde Dominante 7 b13 (#9, #11) en concepto de Piano Solo Voicing:

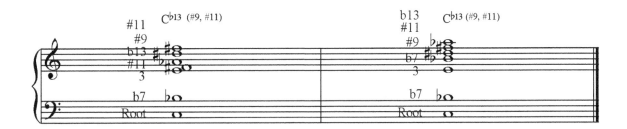

✓ Examples of Dominant 7 b13 (#9, #11) on Ensemble voicing concept/ Ejemplos de un acorde Dominante 7 b13 (#9, #11) en concepto de Ensamble Voicing:

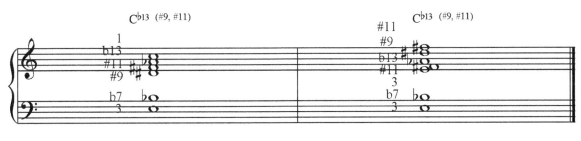

Minor Chords

- A **minor 7th** chord construction is root, b3rd, 5th & b7th

✓ Here we have Cm7 as an example.

- La construcción de un acorde **menor 7** es raíz, b3ra, 5ta & b7ma.

✓ Aquí tenemos como ejemplo el acorde de Cm7.

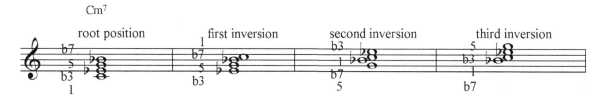

✓ Examples of a Minor 7th chord on Solo Piano concept/ Ejemplos de un acorde Menor 7ma en concepto de Piano Solo Voicing:

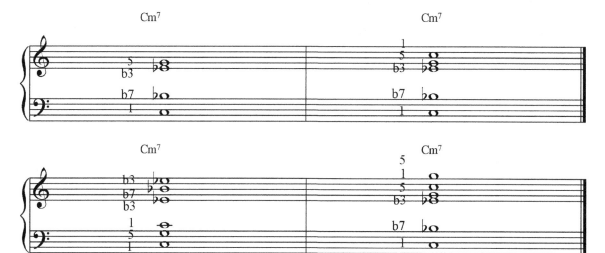

✓ Examples of a Minor 7th chord on Ensemble voicing concept/ Ejemplos de un acorde Menor 7ma en concepto de Ensamble voicing:

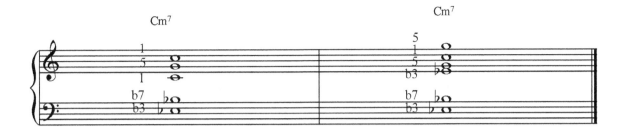

- A **minor Maj7th** chord construction is root, b3rd, 5th & 7th

✓ Here we have Cm Maj7 as an example.

- La construcción del acorde **menor 7ma Mayor** es raíz, b3ra, 5ta & 7ma.

✓ Aquí tenemos como ejemplo el acorde de Cm Maj7.

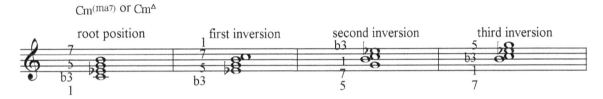

✓ Examples of a Minor major 7th chord on Solo Piano concept/ Ejemplos de un acorde Menor 7ma Mayor en concepto de Piano Solo Voicing:

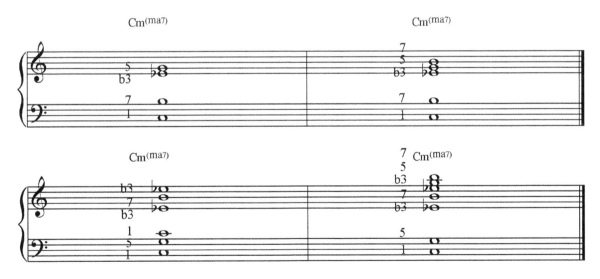

✓ Examples of a Minor major 7th chord on Ensemble voicing concept/ Ejemplos de un acorde Menor 7major en concepto de Ensamble voicing:

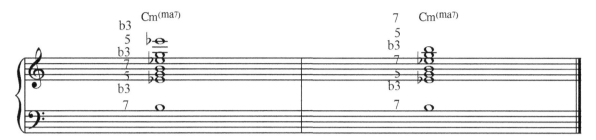

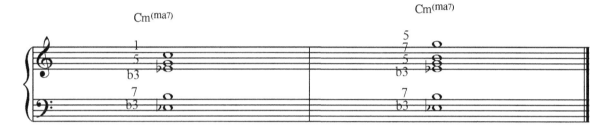

- A **minor7 (9)** chord construction is root, b3rd, 5th, b7th & 9th.

✓ Here we have Cm7 (9) as an example.

- La construcción del acorde **menor7 (9)** es raíz, b3ra, 5ta, b7ma & 9na.

✓ Aquí tenemos como ejemplo el acorde de Cm7 (9)

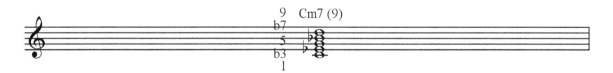

✓ Examples of a minor 7th (9) chord on Solo Piano concept/ Ejemplos de un acorde menor 7 (9) en concepto de Piano Solo Voicing:

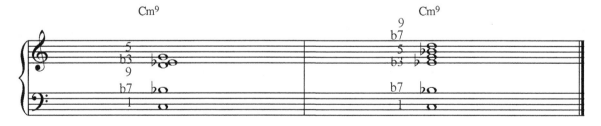

✓ Examples of a minor 7th (9) chord on Ensemble voicing concept/ Ejemplos de un acorde menor 7 (9) en concepto de Ensamble voicing:

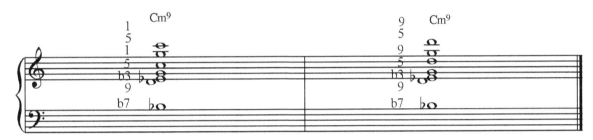

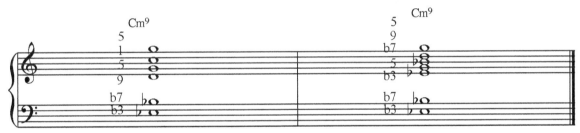

- A **minor Maj7 (9)** chord construction is root, b3rd, 5th, 7th & 9th.

✓ Here we have Cm Maj7 (9) as an example.

- La construcción del acorde **menor Maj7 (9)** es raíz, b3ra, 5ta, 7ma & 9na.

✓ Aquí tenemos como ejemplo el acorde de Cm Maj7 (9)

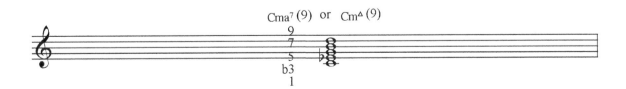

✓ Examples of a minor Major 7th (9) chord on Solo Piano concept/ Ejemplos de un acorde menor 7 Mayor (9) en concepto de Piano Solo Voicing:

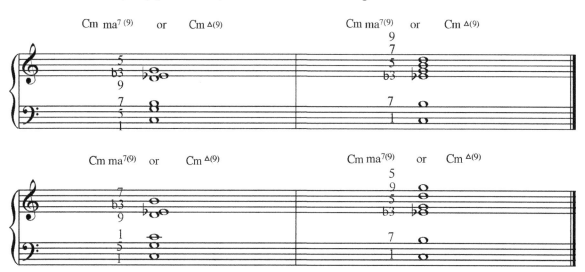

✓ Examples of a minor Major 7th (9) chord on Ensemble voicing concept/ Ejemplos de un acorde menor 7 Mayor (9) en concepto de Ensamble voicing:

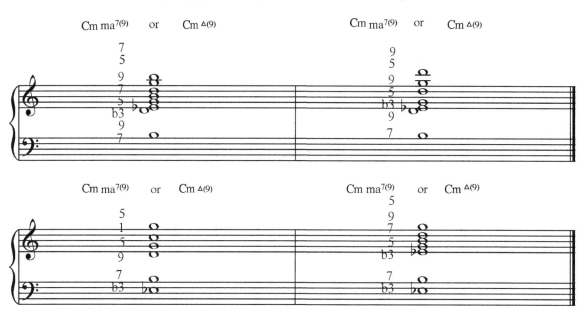

- **A minor7 11th** Chord construction is root, b3rd, 5th, b7th & 11th but on the following example we are adding the 9th

✓ Here we have Cm7 (11) as an example.

- La construcción del acorde **min7 (11**) es raíz, b3, 5ta, b7ma & 11na pero en el siguiente ejemplo estamos agregando la 9na.

✓ Aquí tenemos como ejemplo el acorde de Cm7 (11)

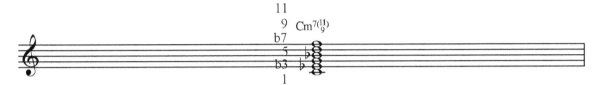

✓ Examples of a minor 7th (11th) chord on Solo Piano concept/ Ejemplos de un acorde menor 7 (11) en concepto de Piano Solo Voicing:

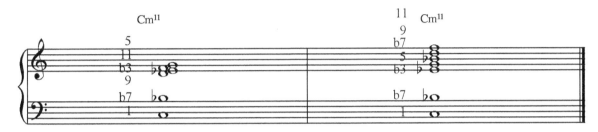

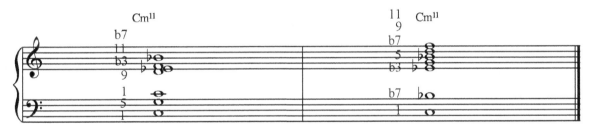

✓ Examples of a minor 7th (11th) chord on Ensemble voicing concept/ Ejemplos de un acorde menor 7 (11) en concepto de Ensamble voicing:

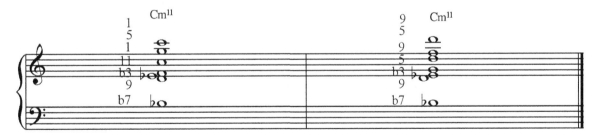

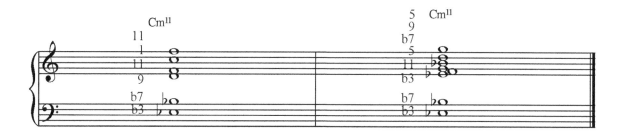

- A **minor7 #11th** chord construction is root, b3rd, 5th, b7th & #11th but on the following example we are adding the 9th

✓ Here we have Cm7 (#11) as an example.

- La construcción del acorde **min7 #11** es raíz, b3, 5ta, b7ma & #11na pero en el siguiente ejemplo estamos agregando la 9na.

✓ Aquí tenemos como ejemplo el acorde de Cm7 (#11)

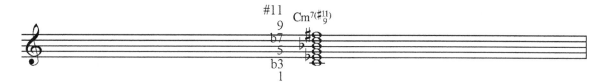

✓ Examples of a minor 7th (#11th) chord on Solo Piano concept/ Ejemplos de un acorde menor 7 (#11) en concepto de Piano Solo Voicing:

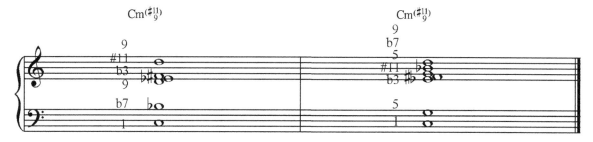

✓ Examples of a minor 7th (#11th) chord on Ensemble voicing concept/ Ejemplos de un acorde menor 7 (#11) en concepto de Ensemble voicing:

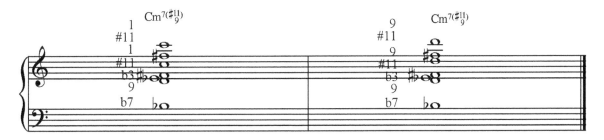

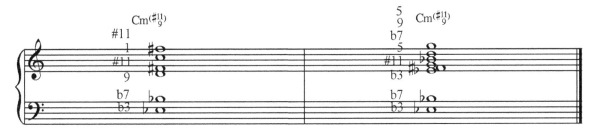

- A **minor Maj7 11th** chord construction is root, b3rd, 5th, 7th & 11th but on the following example we are adding the 9th.

✓ Here we have Cm Maj7 (11) as an example.

- La construcción del acorde **min Maj7 11** es raíz, b3, 5ta, 7ma & 11na pero en el siguiente ejemplo estamos agregando la 9na.

✓ Aquí tenemos como ejemplo el acorde de Cm Maj7 (11)

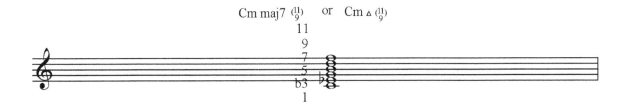

✓ Examples of a minor Major 7th (11th) chord on Solo Piano concept/ Ejemplos de un acorde menor 7 Mayor (11) en concepto de Piano Solo Voicing:

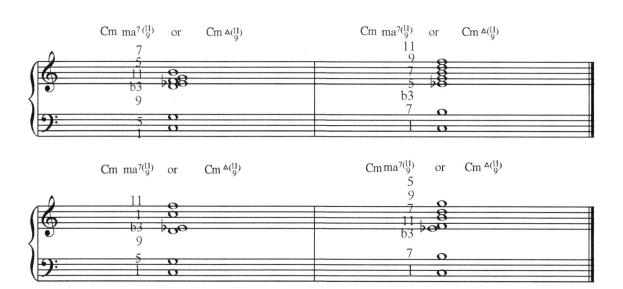

✓ Examples of a minor Major 7th (11th) chord on Ensemble voicing concept/ Ejemplos de un acorde menor 7 Mayor (11) en concepto de Ensamble voicing:

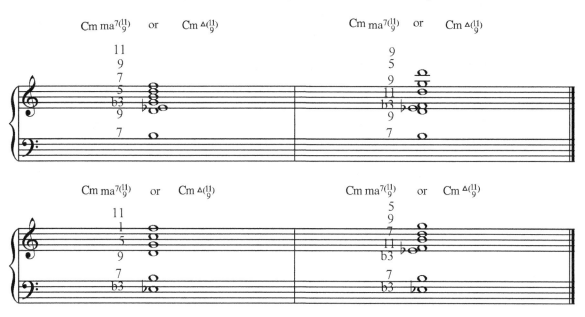

- A **minor Maj7 #11th** chord construction is root, b3rd, 5th, 7th & #11th but on the following example we are adding the 9th.

✓ Here we have Cm Maj7 (#11) as an example.

- La construcción del acorde **min Maj7 #11** es raíz, b3, 5ta, 7ma & #11na pero en el siguiente ejemplo estamos agregando la 9na.

✓ Aquí tenemos como ejemplo el acorde de Cm Maj7 (#11)

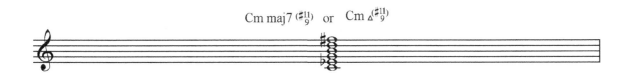

✓ Examples of a minor Major 7th (#11th) chord on Solo Piano concept/ Ejemplos de un acorde menor 7 Mayor (#11) en concepto de Piano Solo Voicing:

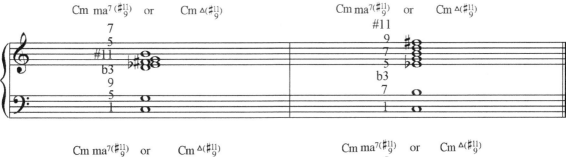

✓ Examples of a minor Major 7th (#11th) chord on Ensemble voicing concept/ Ejemplos de un acorde menor 7 Mayor (#11) en concepto de Ensamble voicing:

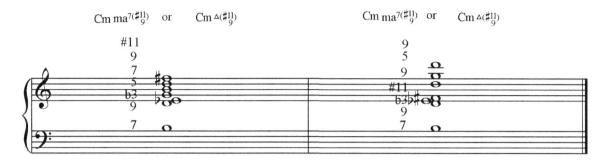

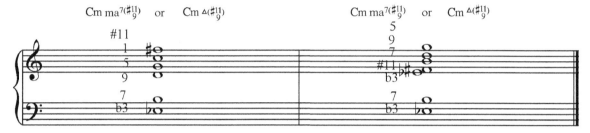

- A **minor 7th (13th, 11th, 9th)** chord construction is root, b3rd, 5th, b7th, 9th, 11th & 13th.

- La construcción de un acorde menor 7 (13, 11, 9) es raíz, b3ra, 5ta, b7ma, 9na, 11na & 13na.

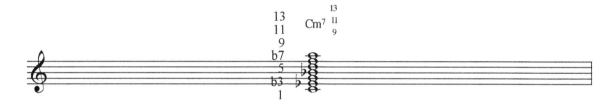

✓ Examples of a minor 7th (13th, 11th, 9th) chord on Solo Piano concept/ Ejemplos de un acorde menor 7 (13, 11, 9) en concepto de Piano Solo Voicing:

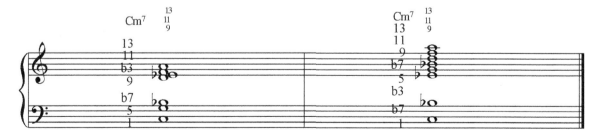

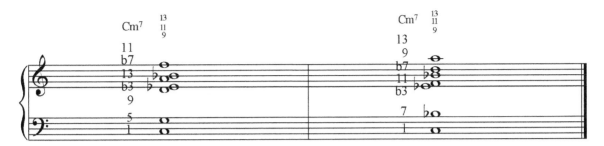

✓ Examples of a minor 7th (13th) chord on Ensemble voicing concept/ Ejemplos de un acorde menor 7 (13) en concepto de Ensamble voicing:

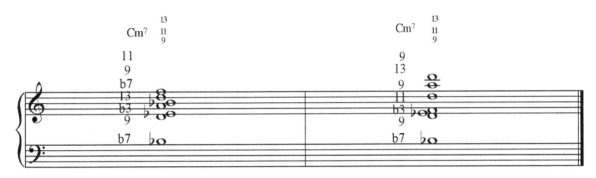

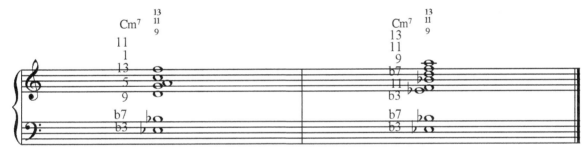

- A **minor 7th (13th, #11th, 9th)** chord construction is root, b3rd, 5th, b7th, 9th, #11th & 13th.

- La construcción de un acorde **menor 7 (13, #11, 9)** es raíz, b3ra, 5ta, b7ma, 9na, #11na & 13na.

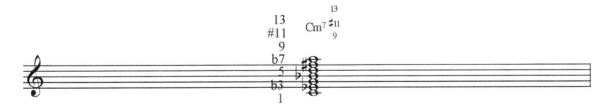

39

✓ Examples of a minor 7th (13th ,#11th , 9th) chord on Solo Piano concept/Ejemplos de un acorde menor 7 (13, #11, 9) en concepto de Piano Solo Voicing:

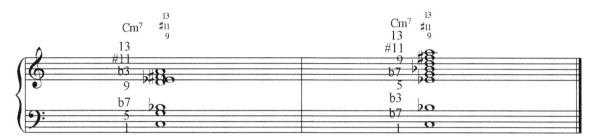

✓ Examples of a minor 7th (13th ,#11th , 9th) chord on Ensemble voicing concept/ Ejemplos de un acorde menor 7 (13, #11, 9) en concepto de Ensamble voicing:

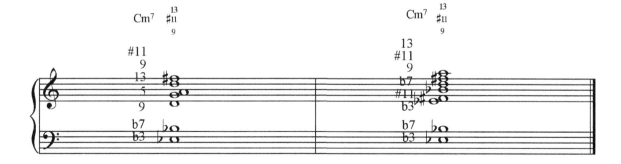

- A **Minor Maj7th (13th, 11th, 9th)** chord construction is root, b3rd, 5th, 7th, 9th, 11th & 13th.

- La construcción de un acorde **Menor Ma7 (13, 11, 9)** es raíz, b3ra, 5ta, 7ma, 9na, 11na & 13na.

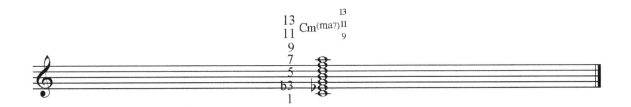

- ✓ Examples of a minor ma7th (13th ,11th , 9th) chord on Solo Piano concept/ Ejemplos de un acorde menor ma7 (13, 11, 9) en concepto de Piano Solo Voicing:

- ✓ Examples of a minor ma7th (13th ,11th , 9th) chord on Ensemble voicing concept/ Ejemplos de un acorde menor ma7 (13, 11, 9) en concepto de Ensamble voicing:

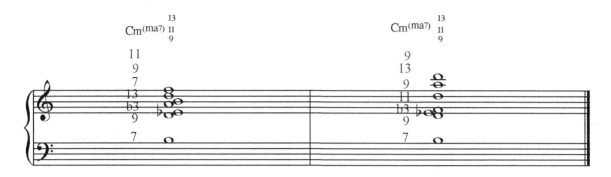

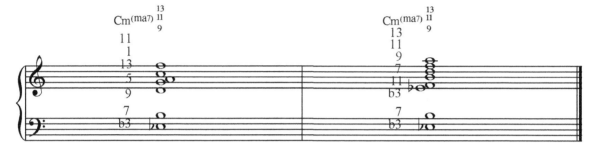

- A **minor maj7th (13th, #11th, 9th)** chord construction is root, b3rd, 5th, 7th, 9th, #11th & 13th.

- La construcción de un **acorde menor ma7 (13, #11, 9)** es raíz, b3ra, 5ta, 7ma, 9na, #11na & 13na.

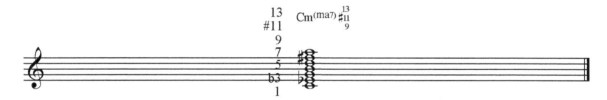

✓ Examples of a minor maj7th (13th ,#11th , 9th) chord on Solo Piano concept/ Ejemplos de un acorde menor ma7 (13, #11, 9) en concepto de Piano Solo Voicing:

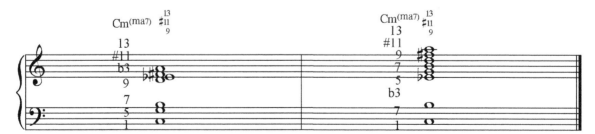

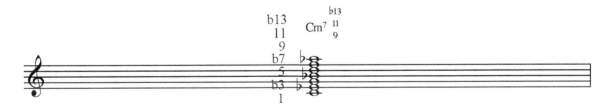

✓ Examples of a minor ma7th (13th ,#11th , 9th) chord on Ensemble voicing concept/ Ejemplos de un acorde menor ma7 (13, #11, 9) en concepto de Ensemble voicing:

- A **minor 7th (b13th, 11th, 9th)** chord construction is root, b3rd, 5th, b7th, 9th, 11th & b13th.

- La construcción de un **acorde menor 7 (b13, 11, 9)** es raíz, b3ra, 5ta, b7ma, 9na, 11na & b13na.

✓ Examples of a minor 7th (b13th, 11th, 9th) chord on Solo Piano concept/ Ejemplos de un acorde menor 7 (b13,11, 9) en concepto de Piano Solo Voicing:

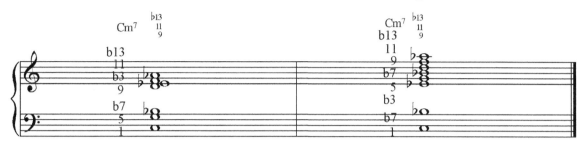

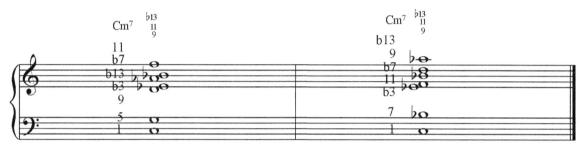

✓ Examples of a minor 7th (b13th, 11th, 9th) chord on Ensemble voicing concept/ Ejemplos de un acorde menor 7 (b13, 11, 9) en concepto de Ensamble Voicing:

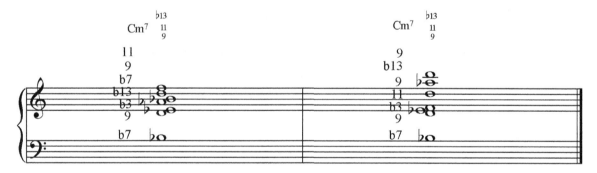

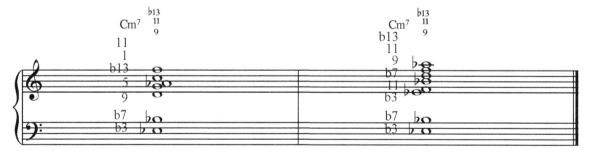

- A **minor 7ᵗʰ (b13ᵗʰ, #11th, 9th)** chord construction is root, b3ʳᵈ, 5ᵗʰ, b7ᵗʰ, 9ᵗʰ, #11ᵗʰ & b13ᵗʰ.

- La construcción de un acorde **menor 7 (b13, #11, 9)** es raíz, b3ra, 5ta, b7ma, 9na, #11na & b13na.

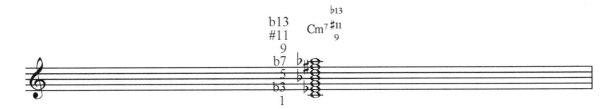

✓ Examples of a minor 7ᵗʰ (b13ᵗʰ ,#11ᵗʰ , 9ᵗʰ) chord on Solo Piano concept/ Ejemplos de un acorde menor 7 (b13, #11, 9) en concepto de Piano Solo voicing:

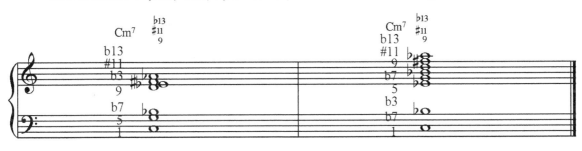

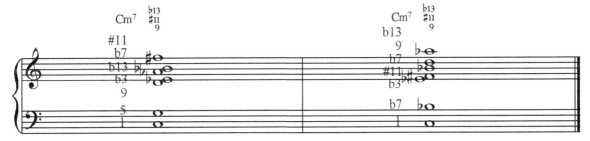

✓ Examples of a minor 7th (b13th ,#11th , 9th) chord on Ensemble voicing concept/ Ejemplos de un acorde menor 7 (b13, #11, 9) en concepto de Ensemble voicing:

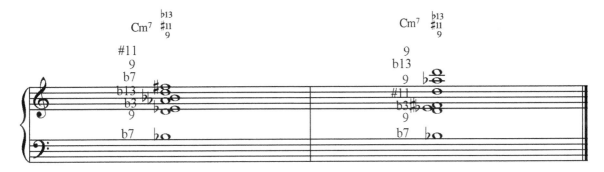

45

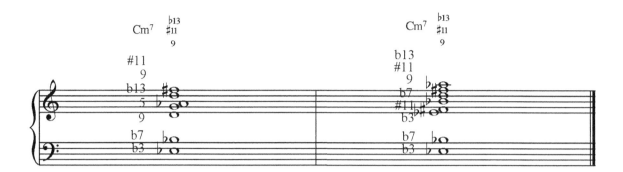

- A **minor ma7th (b13th, 11th, 9th)** chord construction is root, b3rd, 5th, 7th, 9th, 11th & b13th.

- La construcción de un acorde **menor ma7 (b13, 11, 9)** es raíz, b3ra, 5ta, 7ma, 9na, 11na & b13na.

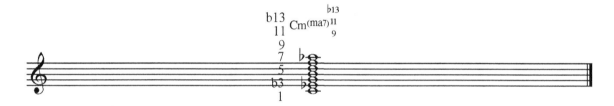

✓ Examples of a minor ma7th (b13th ,11th , 9th) chord on Solo Piano concept/ Ejemplos de un acorde menor ma7 (b13, 11, 9) en concepto de Piano Solo voicing:

✓ Examples of a minor ma7th (b13th ,11th , 9th) chord on Ensemble voicing concept/
  Ejemplos de un acorde menor ma7 (b13, 11, 9) en concepto de Ensamble voicing:

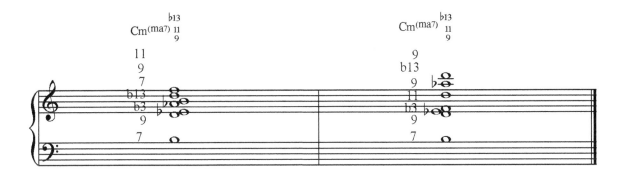

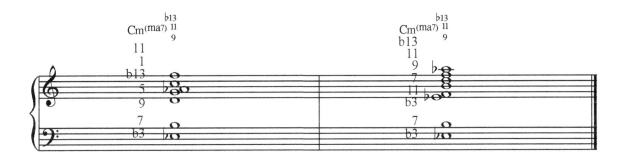

- A **minor ma7th (b13th, #11th, 9th)** chord construction is root, b3rd, 5th, 7th, 9th, #11th & b13th.

- La construcción de un acorde **menor ma7 (b13, #11, 9)** es raíz, b3ra, 5ta, 7ma, 9na, #11na & b13na.

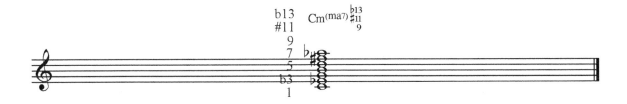

✓ Examples of a minor ma7th (b13th ,#11th , 9th) chord on Solo Piano concept/ Ejemplos de un acorde menor ma7 (b13, #11, 9) en concepto de Piano Solo Voicing:

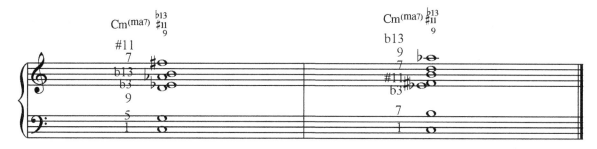

✓ Examples of a minor ma7th (b13th ,#11th , 9th) chord on Ensemble voicing concept/ Ejemplos de un acorde menor ma7 (b13, #11, 9) en concepto de Ensamble voicing:

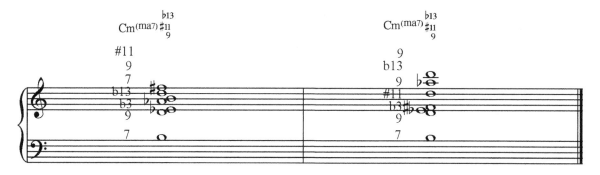

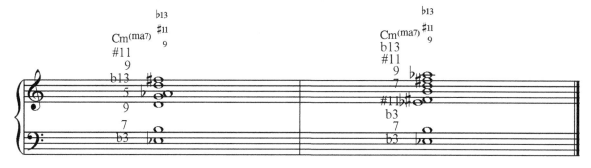

- **C half diminished**, Cm7 (b5) or C Ø chord construction is root, b3rd, b5th & b7th

- La construcción del acorde **C semi disminuido**, Cm7 (b5) o C Ø es raíz, 3ra, b5ta & b7ma.

- ✓ Examples of a half diminished, Cm7 (b5) or C Ø chord on Solo Piano concept/ Ejemplos de un acorde semi disminuido, Cm7 (b5) o C Ø en concepto de Piano Solo Voicing:

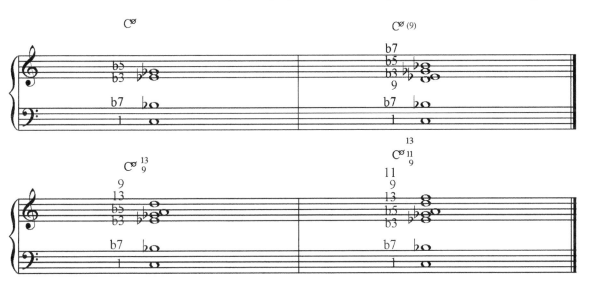

- ✓ Examples of a half diminished, Cm7 (b5) or C Ø chord on Ensemble voicing concept/ Ejemplos de un acorde semi disminuido, Cm7 (b5) o C Ø en concepto de Ensamble voicing:

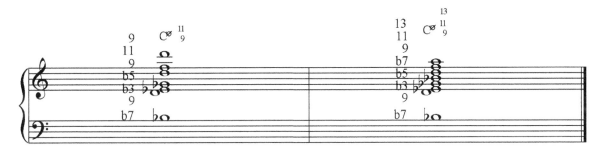

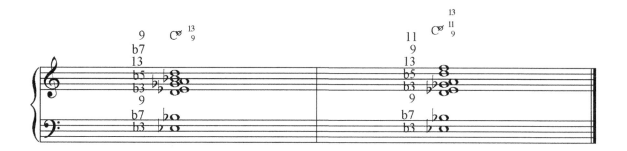

- C half-diminished maj7th, Cmb5 maj7th or C Ø maj7th chord construction is root, b3rd, b5th & 7th

- La construcción del acorde C semi disminuido 7ma mayor es raíz, b3ra, b5ta & 7ma.

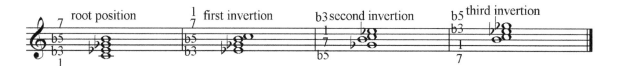

✓ Examples of a half diminished maj7th, Cm7 b5 maj7th or C Ø maj7th chord on Solo Piano concept/ Ejemplos de un acorde semi disminuido, Cm7 b5 maj7th o C Ø maj7th en concepto de Piano Solo Voicing:

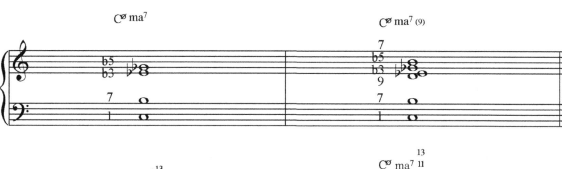

✓ Examples of a half diminished maj7th, Cm7 b5 maj7th or C Ø maj7th chord on Ensemble voicing concept/ Ejemplos de un acorde semi disminuido maj7th , Cm7 b5 maj7th o C Ø maj7th en concepto de Ensamble Voicing:

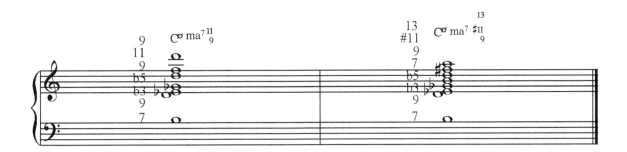

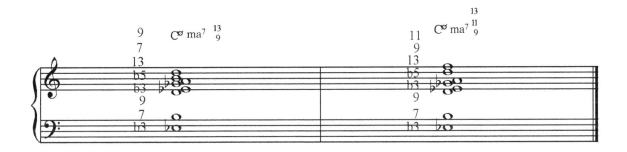

C Major Scale & Its Modes/ La Escala Mayor de Do y sus Modos

A **Mode** is type of scale created by establishing a new tonic within a preexisting scale.

Un **Modo** es el tipo de escala donde cada nota establece una nueva tónica dentro de la escala establecida.

Ionian/Major Scale/Escala Mayor

C Maj7 or C △

Dorian

Dorian is the second mode of a major scale & its chord quality is a **Minor 7th Chord**

Dorian es el Segundo modo de una escala mayor y el acorde que lo acompaña es un **Menor 7ma**

Dm7

Phrygian

Phrygian is the third mode of a major scale & its chord quality is a 3rd with a 1/2 step triad above.

Phrygian es el tercer modo de una escala mayor y el acorde que lo acompaña es la 3ra con una triada de 1/2 tono arriba.

F/E

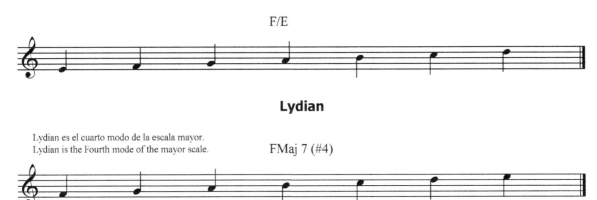

Lydian

Lydian es el cuarto modo de la escala mayor.
Lydian is the Fourth mode of the mayor scale.

FMaj 7 (#4)

Mixolydian

Mixolydian is the fifth mode of the major scale.
Mixolydian es el quinto modo de la escala mayor.

G7

Aeolian

Aeolian is the sixth mode of the major scale.
Aeolian is the sixth mode of the major scale.

Am7(b6)

Locrian

Locrian is the seventh mode of the major scale.
Locrian es el septimo modo de la escala mayor.

Bm7(b5) or B ∅

C Major Scale Modes & Its Chord Changes

Ionian/ C Maj7

This is an example of a C Maj7 chord solo Piano concept/ Acorde de C Maj7 estilo de Piano solo.

C Maj7 or C Δ

This is an example of a C Maj7 chord on an ensemble concept; the bass is playing the chord root/ Acorde de C Maj7 en concepto de ensamble; el bajo toca la tónica.

C Maj7 or C Δ

Dorian

This is an example of a Dm7 chord solo Piano concept/ Acorde de Dm7 en concepto de Piano solo.

Dm7

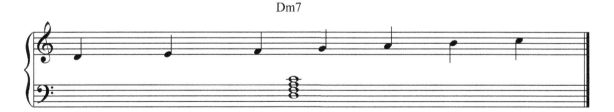

This is an example of a Dm7 chord on an ensemble concept; the bass is playing the chord root.

Acorde de Dm7 en concepto de ensamble; el bajo toca la tónica.

Dm7

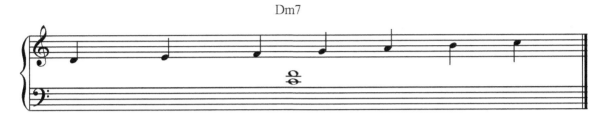

Phrygian

This is an example of E Phrygian chord solo Piano/ ensemble concept. Acorde Phrygian en los dos conceptos.

E Phrygian/ F/E

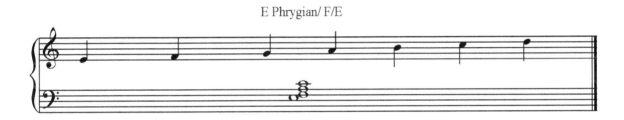

Lydian

This is an example of F Lydian chord solo Piano concept/ Acorde Lydian Piano solo concept.

Fmaj7 #4 or Fmaj7 #11

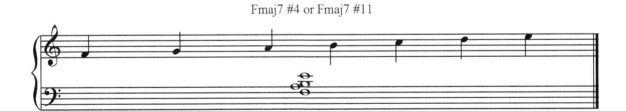

This is an example of F Lydian chord on an ensemble concept; the bass is playing the chord root / Acorde Lydian concepto de ensamble; el bajo toca la tónica.

Fmaj7 #4 or Fmaj7 #11

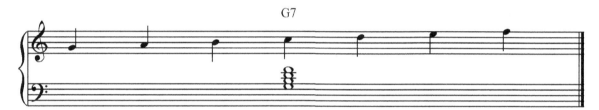

Mixolydian

This is an example of G Mixolydian chord solo Piano concept/ Acorde Mixolydian Piano solo.

G7

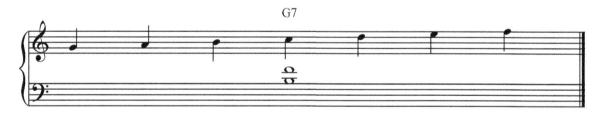

This is an example of G Mixolydian chord on an ensemble concept; the bass is playing the chord root. Acorde Mixolydian concepto de ensamble; el bajo toca la tónica.

G7

This is an example of Am7 (b6) Aeolian chord solo Piano concept/ Acorde Aeolian Piano solo.

Am7(b6)

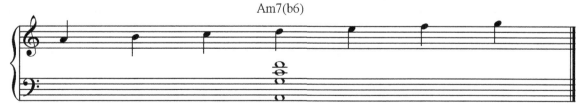

Aeolian

This is an example of Am7 (b6) chord on an ensemble concept; the bass is playing the chord root/ Acorde Aeolian concepto de ensamble; el bajo toca la tónica.

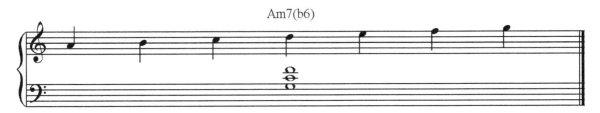

Am7(b6)

Locrian

This is an example of Bm7 (b5) chord solo Piano concept/ Acorde Locrian en concepto de Piano solo.

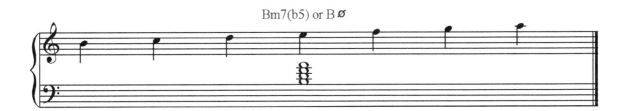

Bm7(b5) or B ∅

This is an example of Bm7 (b5) chord on an ensemble concept; the bass is playing the chord root/ Acorde Locrian en concepto de ensamble; el bajo toca la tónica.

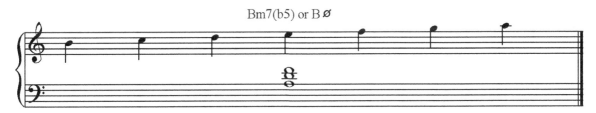

Bm7(b5) or B ∅

Examples of how to use the modes on a 2-5-1 chord progression

Ejemplos de cómo usar los modos en la progresión 2-5-1

EXAMPLES OF ii-V-I (ii m7 - V7 - I M7)

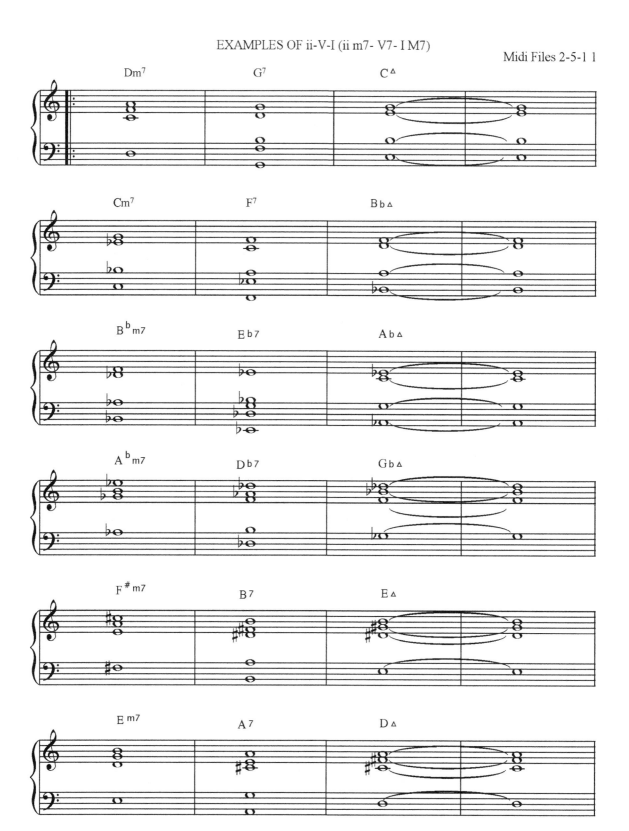

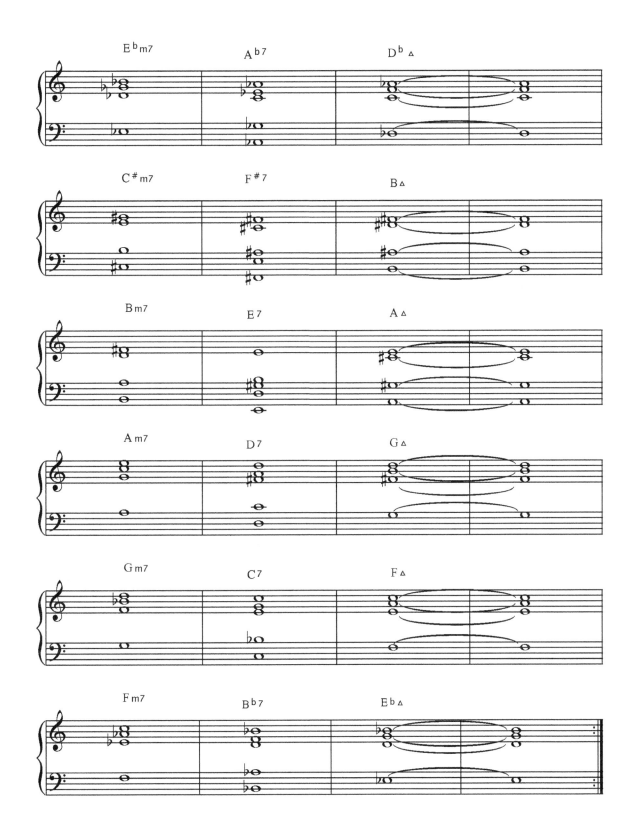

59

EXAMPLES OF ii-V-I (ii m7 - V7 #5 - I M7)

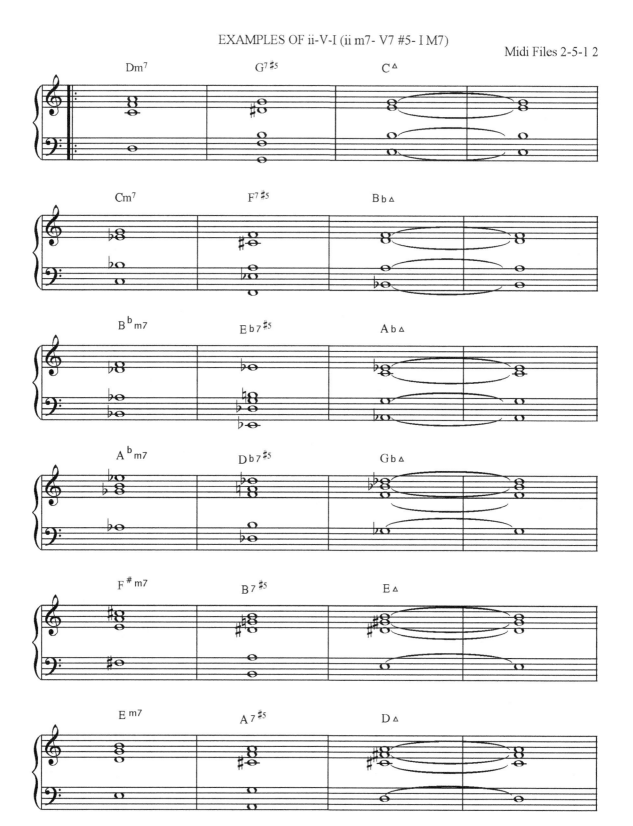

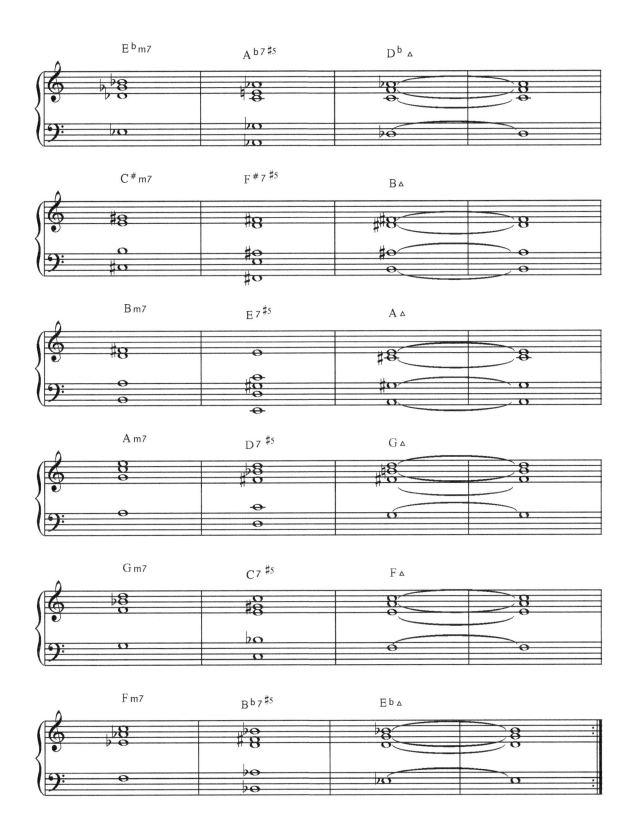

EXAMPLES OF ii-V-I (i m7 9- V7 b9- I M7)

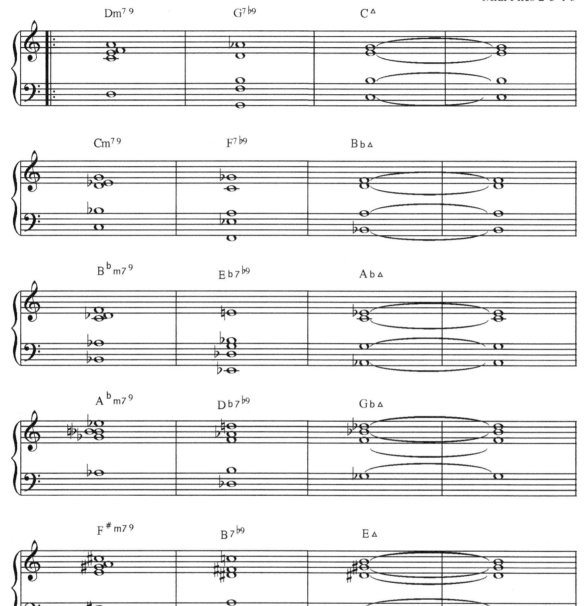

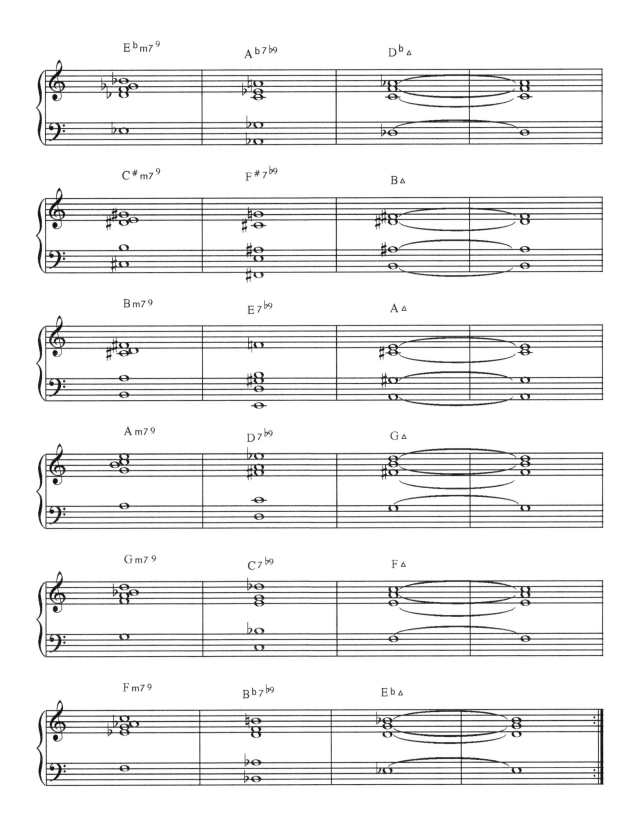

EXAMPLES OF ii-V-I (i m7 9- V7 9- I M7)

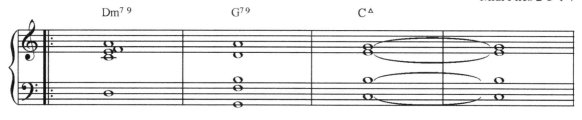

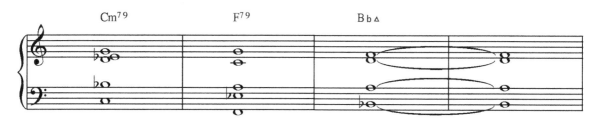

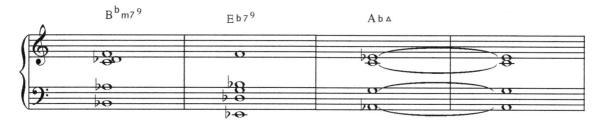

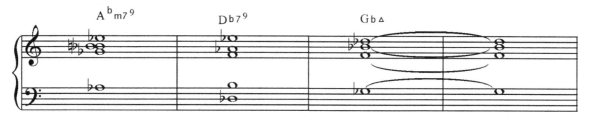

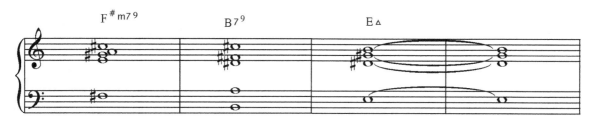

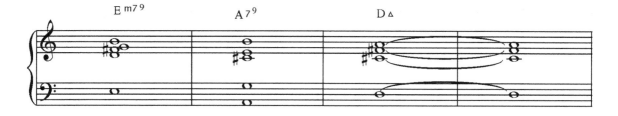

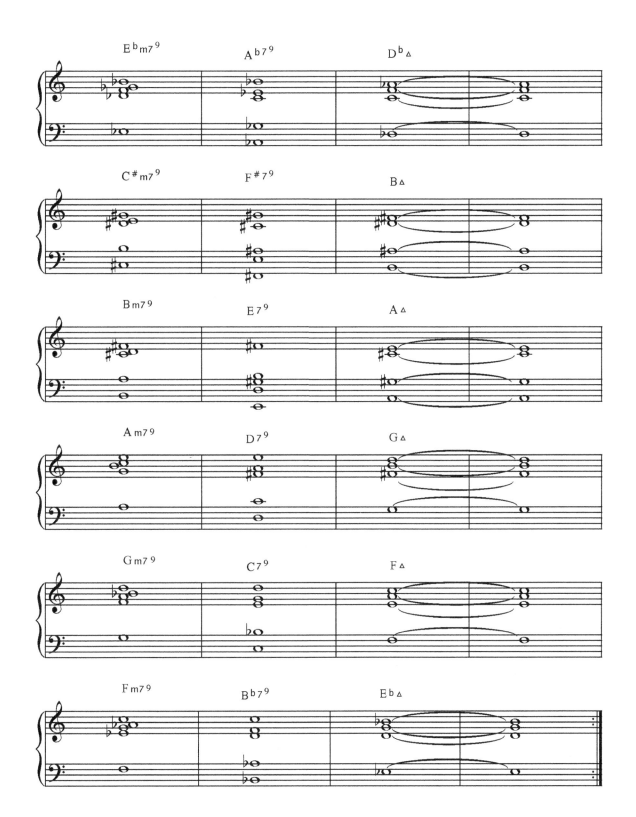

65

EXAMPLES OF ii-V-I (i m7 9- V7 #9- I M7)

Midi Files 2-5-1 5

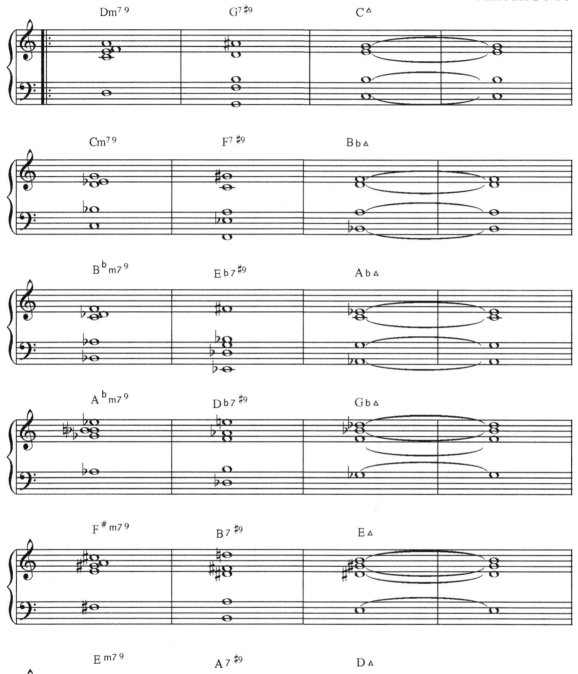

66

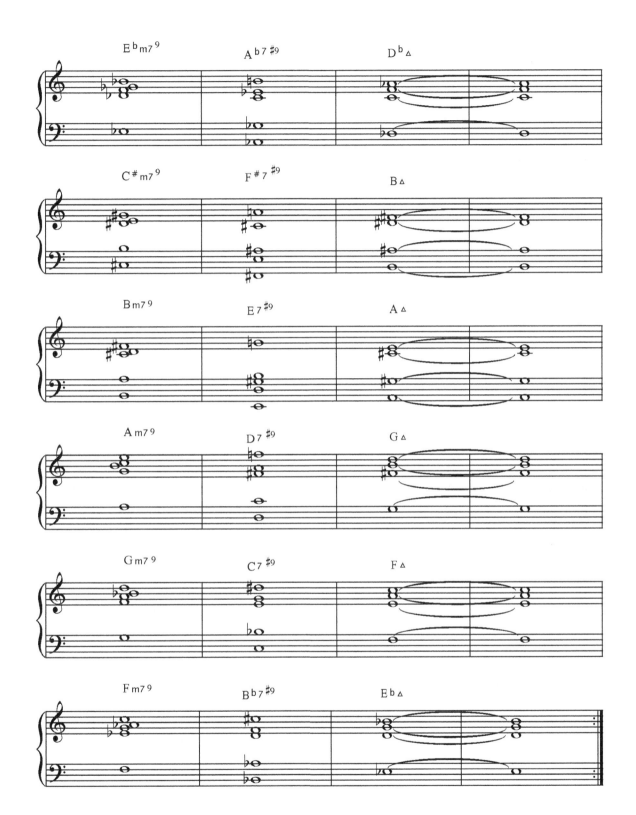

EXAMPLES OF ii-V-I (ii m7 9 11- V7 #5- I M7)

Midi Files 2-5-1 6

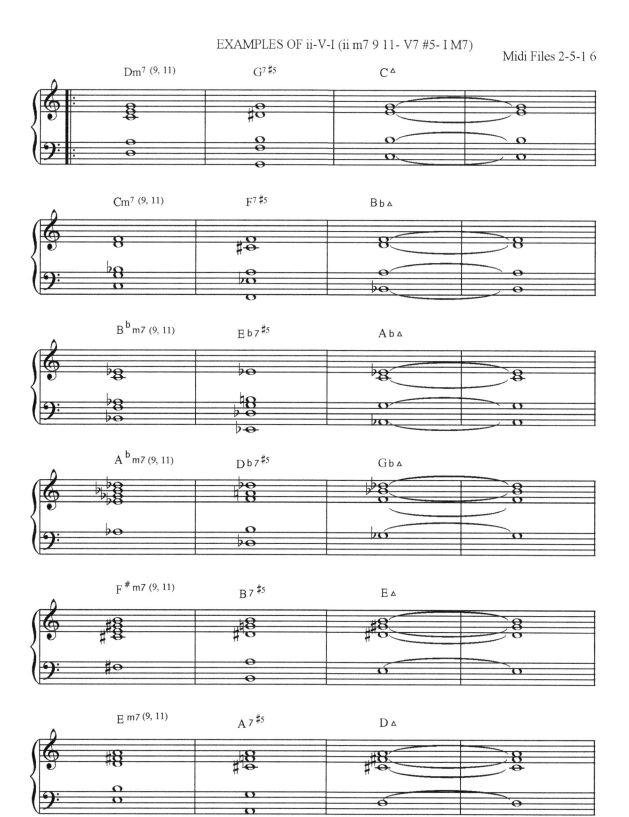

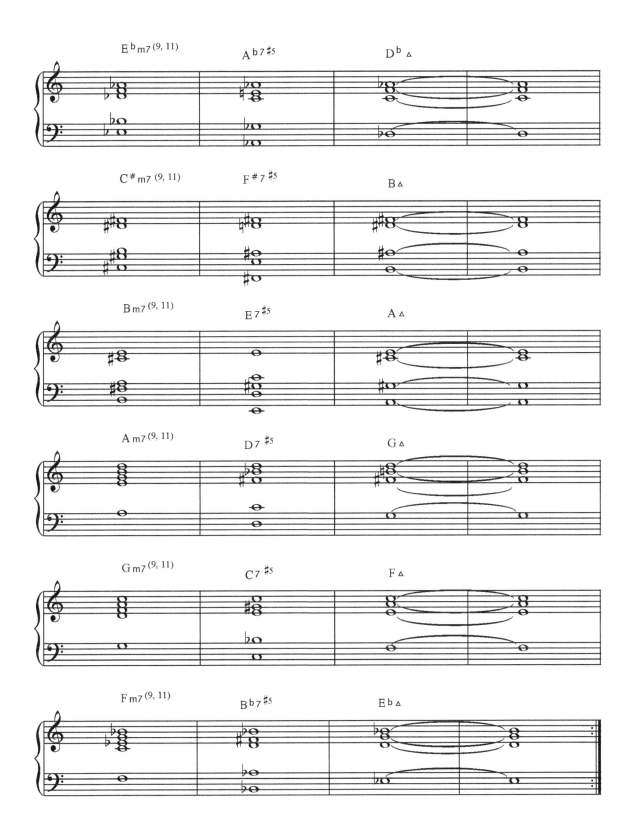

EXAMPLES OF ii-V-I (ii m7 9 11- V7 b9- I M7)

Dm⁷ ⁽⁹, ¹¹⁾   G⁷ ᵇ⁹   C△

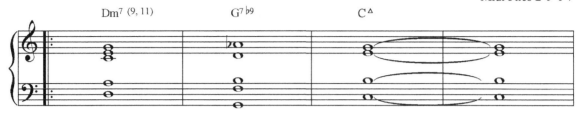

Cm⁷ ⁽⁹, ¹¹⁾   F⁷ ᵇ⁹   Bb△

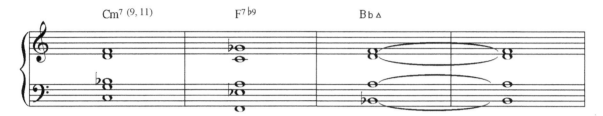

Bᵇ m7 ⁽⁹, ¹¹⁾   E b 7 ᵇ⁹   A b △

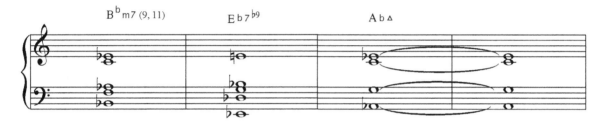

Aᵇ m7 ⁽⁹, ¹¹⁾   D b 7 ᵇ⁹   Gb△

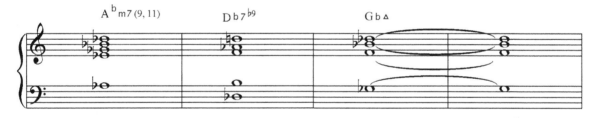

F# m7 ⁽⁹, ¹¹⁾   B 7 ᵇ⁹   E△

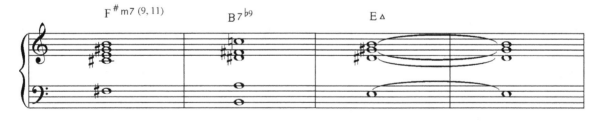

E m7 ⁽⁹, ¹¹⁾   A 7 ᵇ⁹   D△

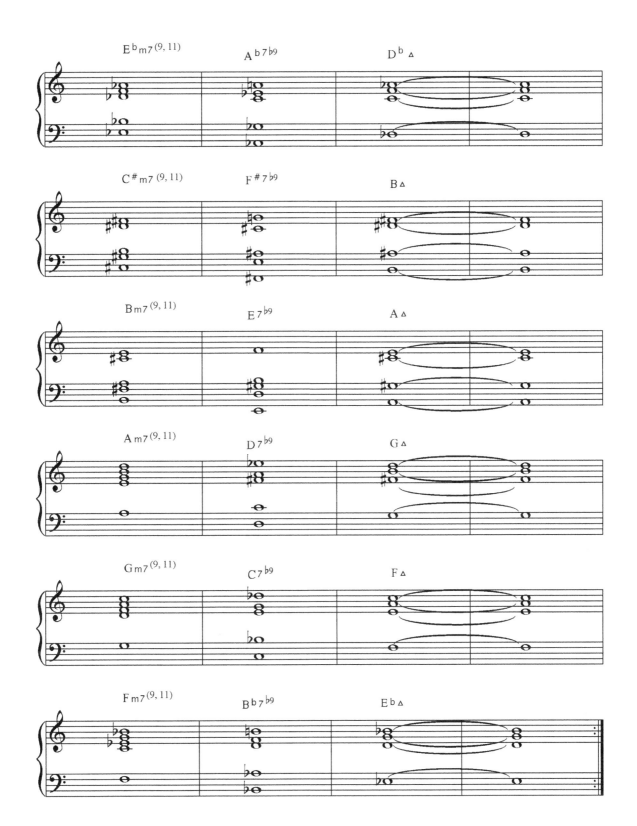

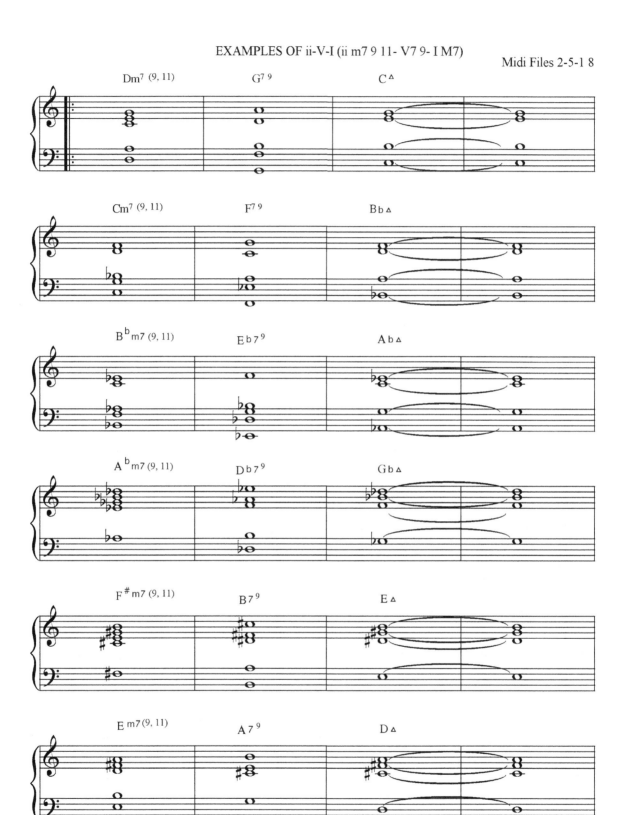

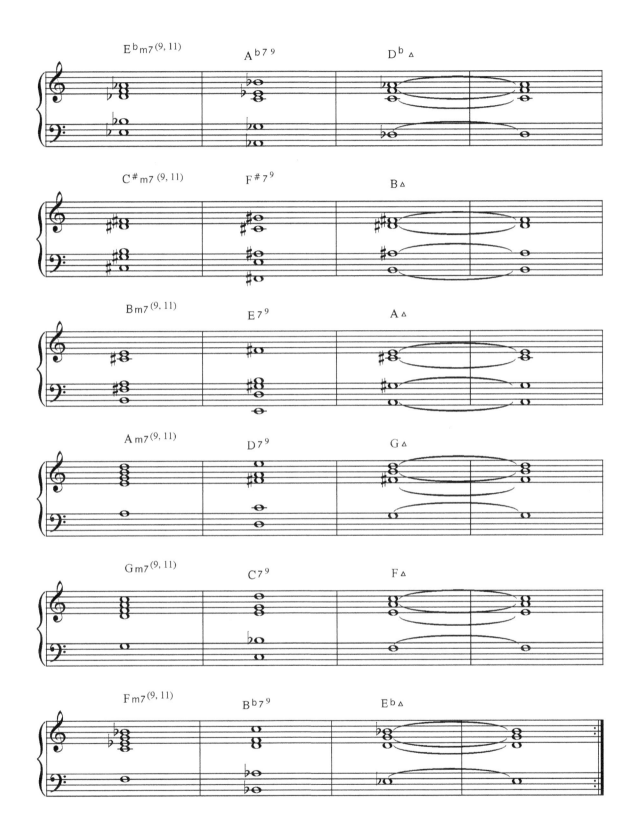

EXAMPLES OF ii-V-I (ii m7 9 11- V7 #9- I M7)

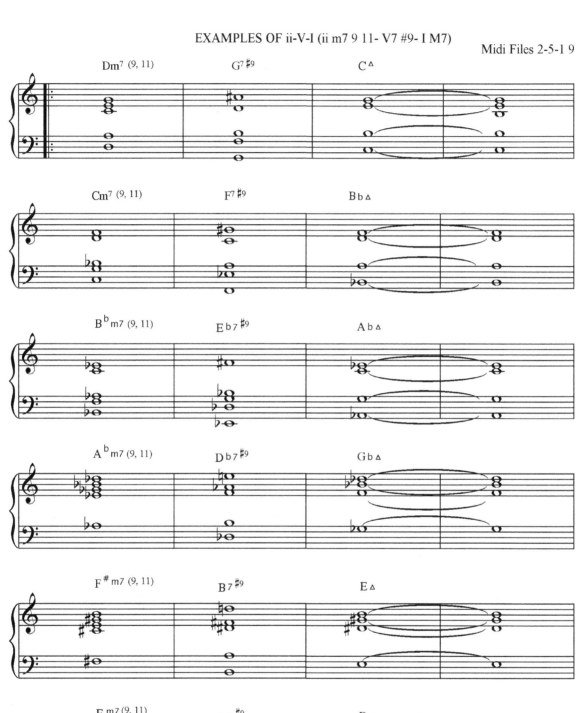

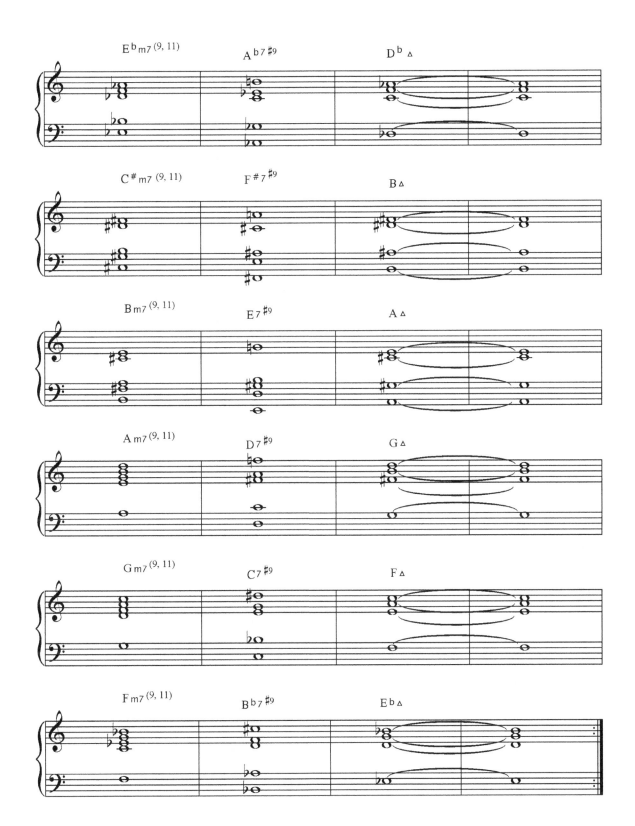

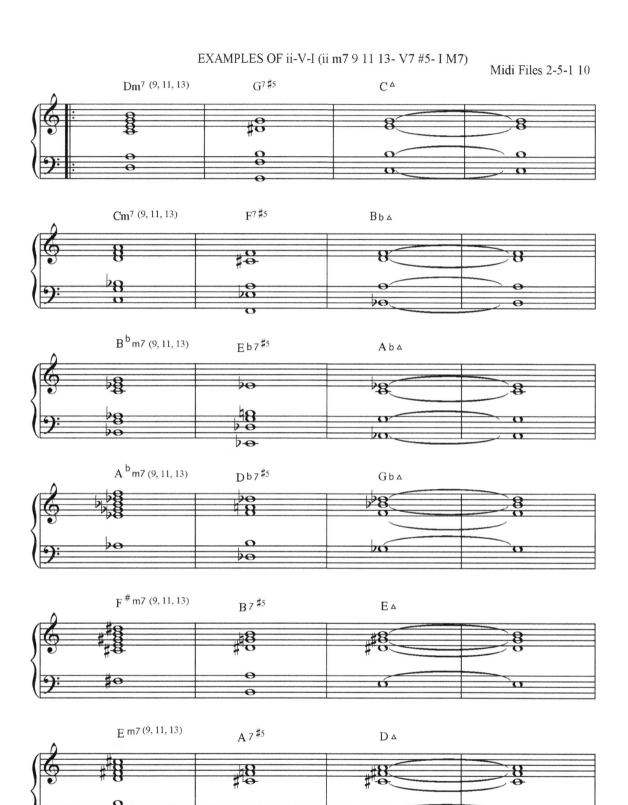

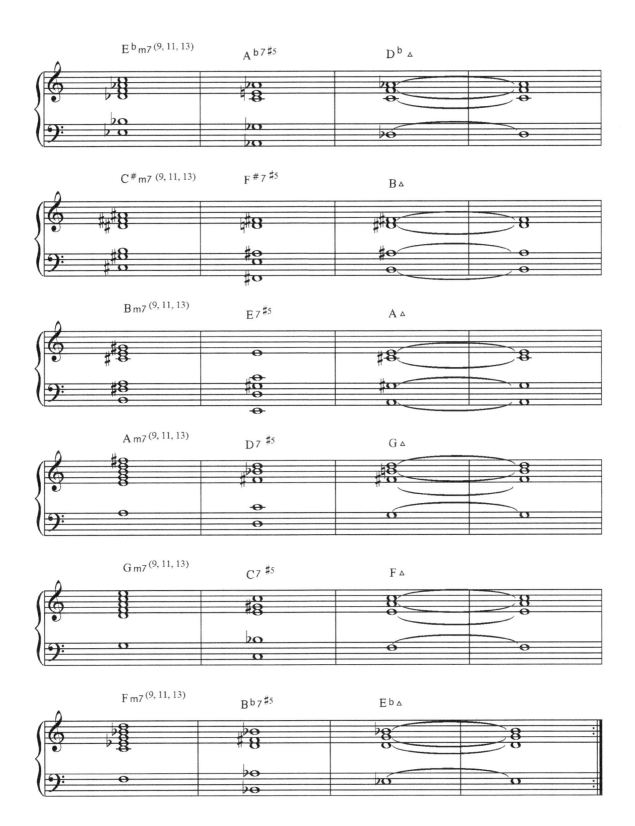

77

EXAMPLES OF ii-V-I (ii m7 9 11 13- V7 b9- I M7)

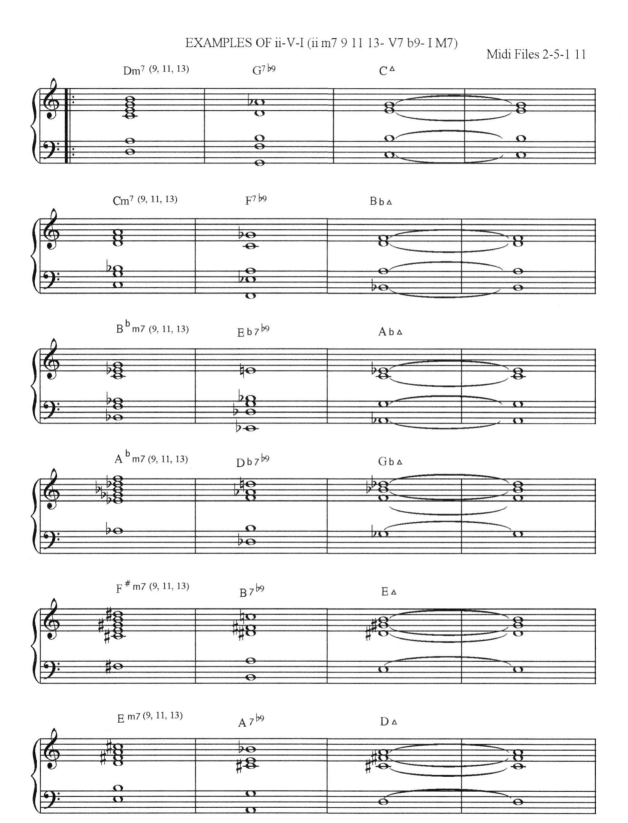

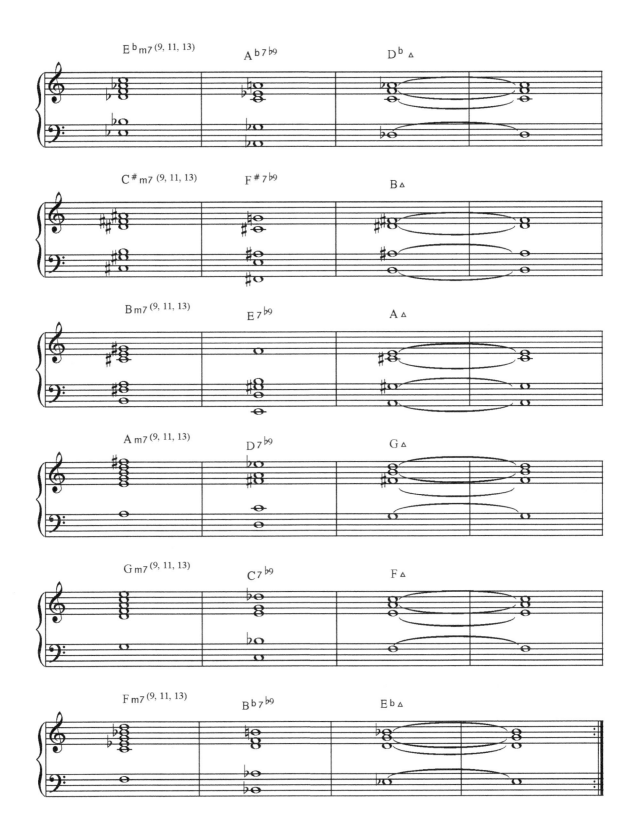

79

EXAMPLES OF ii-V-I (ii m7 9 11 13- V7 9- I M7)

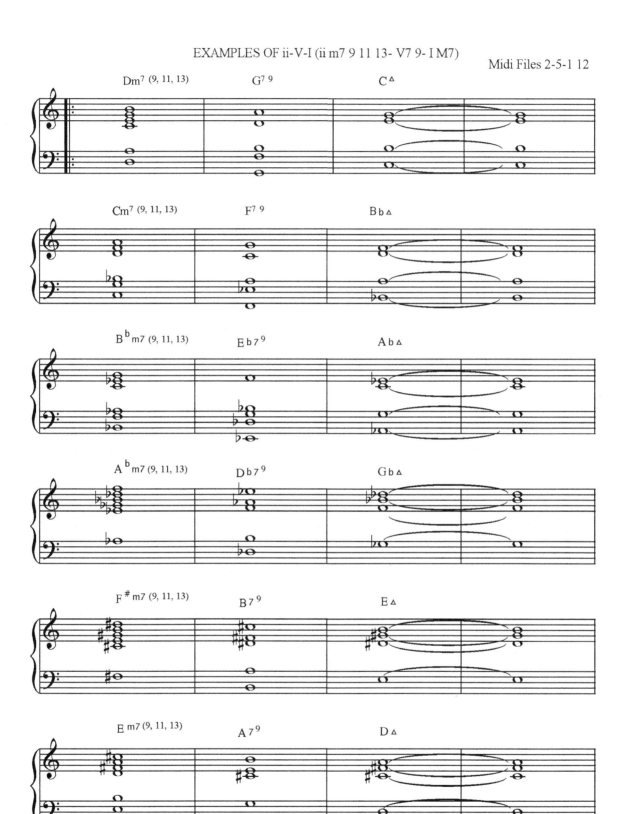

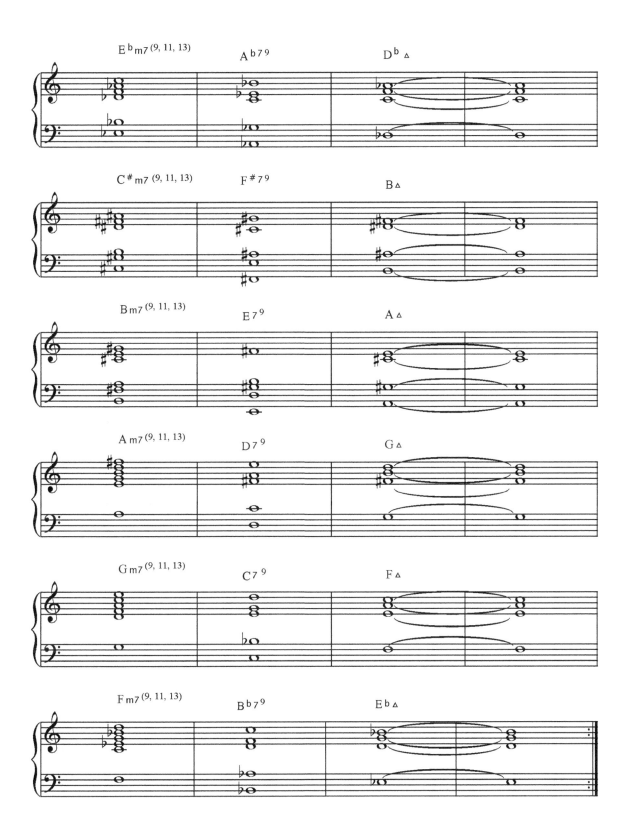

EXAMPLES OF ii-V-I (ii m7 9 11 13- V7 #9- I M7)

Dm⁷ ⁽⁹, ¹¹, ¹³⁾   G⁷ ♯⁹   C △

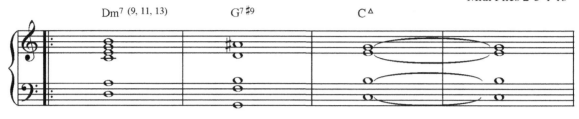

Cm⁷ ⁽⁹, ¹¹, ¹³⁾   F⁷ ♯⁹   Bb △

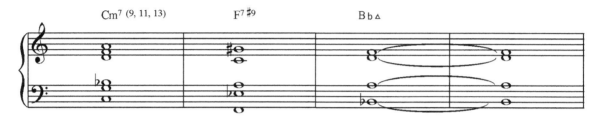

Bᵇm7 ⁽⁹, ¹¹, ¹³⁾   Eb7 ♯⁹   Ab △

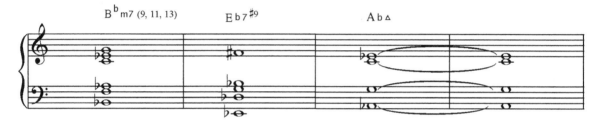

Aᵇm7 ⁽⁹, ¹¹, ¹³⁾   Db7 ♯⁹   Gb △

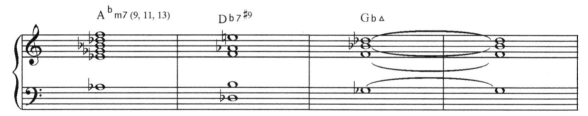

F♯m7 ⁽⁹, ¹¹, ¹³⁾   B7 ♯⁹   E △

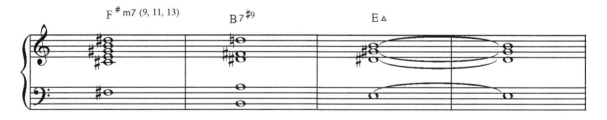

E m7 ⁽⁹, ¹¹, ¹³⁾   A 7 ♯⁹   D △

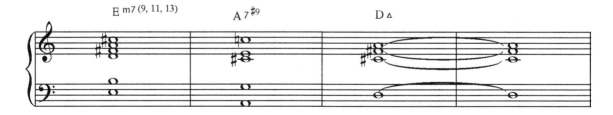

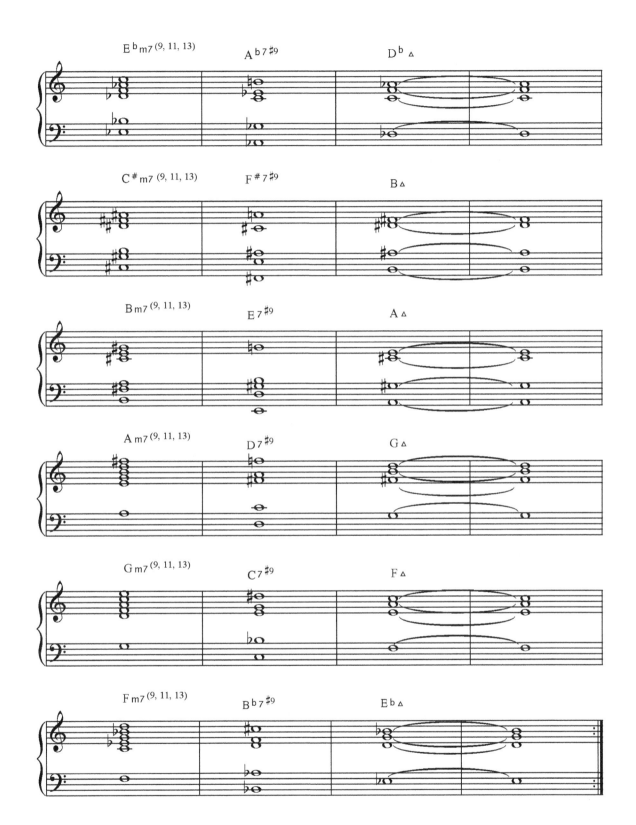

EXAMPLES OF ii-V-I (i m7 9- V 7 b9 #11- I M7)

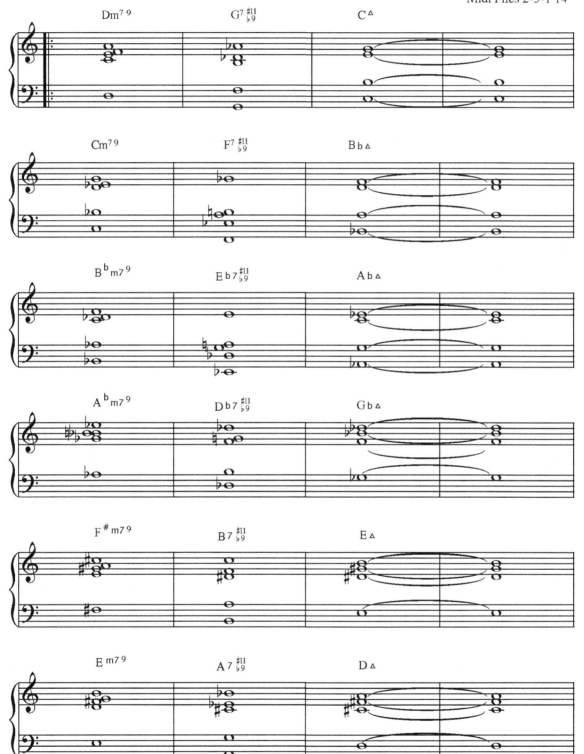

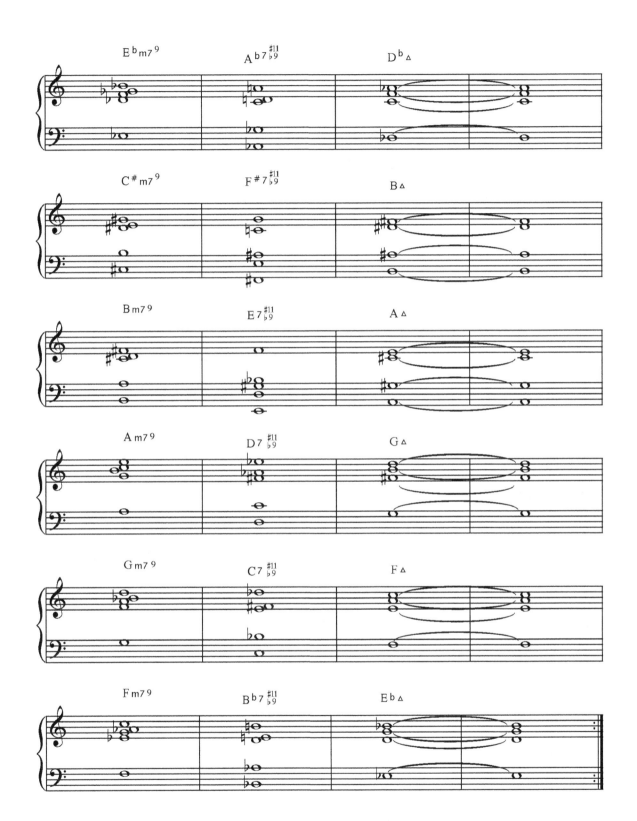

EXAMPLES OF ii-V-I (i m7 9- V7 9 #11- I M7)

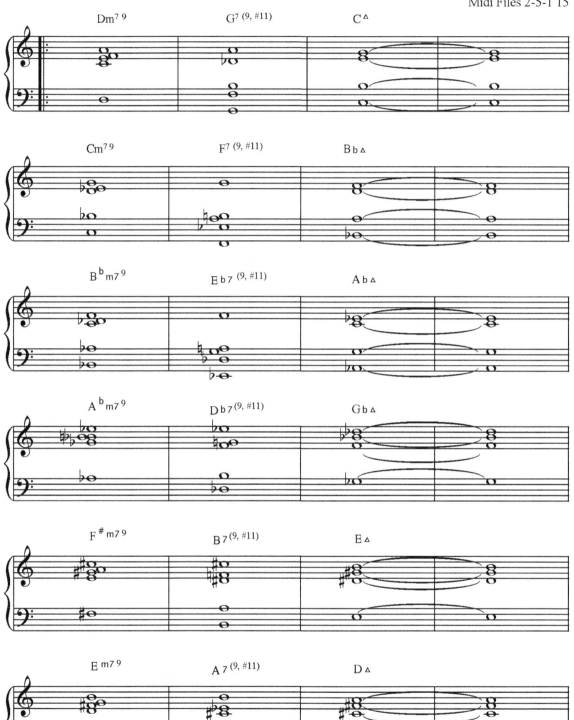

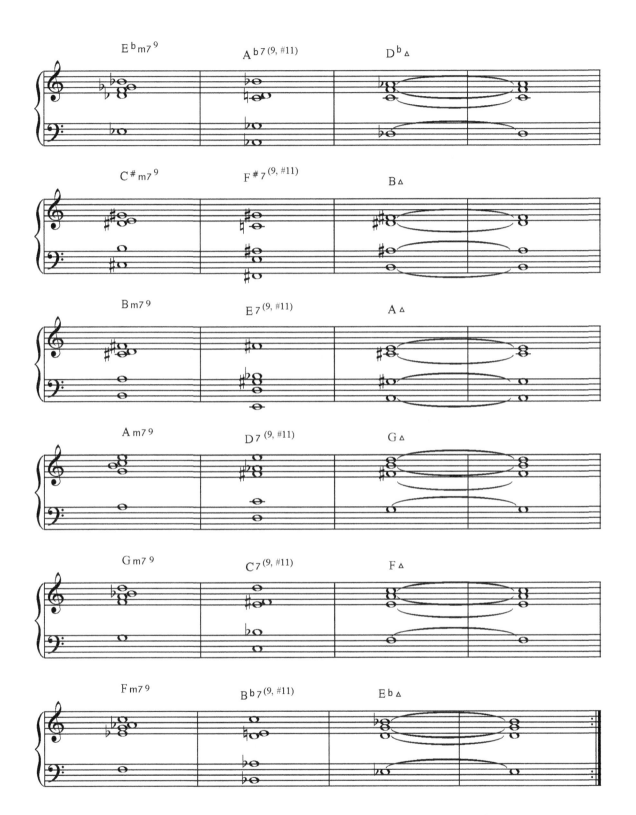

EXAMPLES OF ii-V-I (i m7 9- V7 #9 #11- I M7 9)

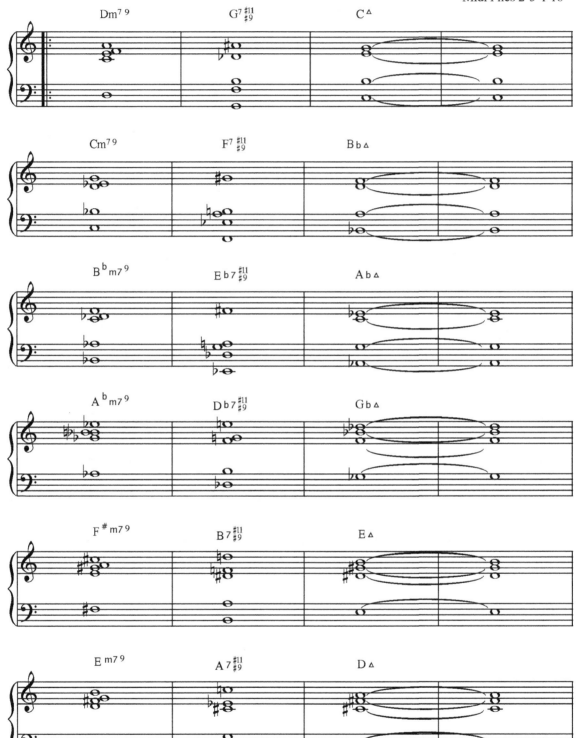

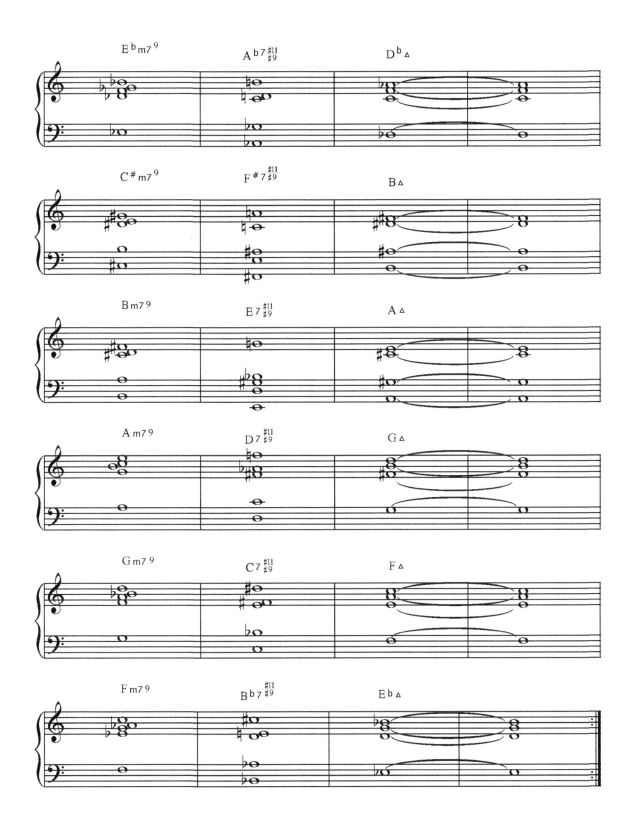

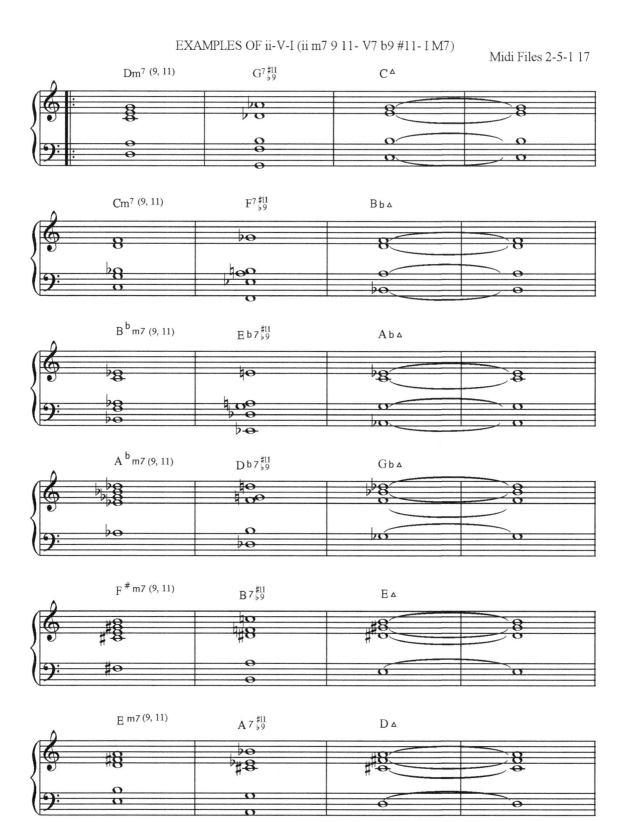

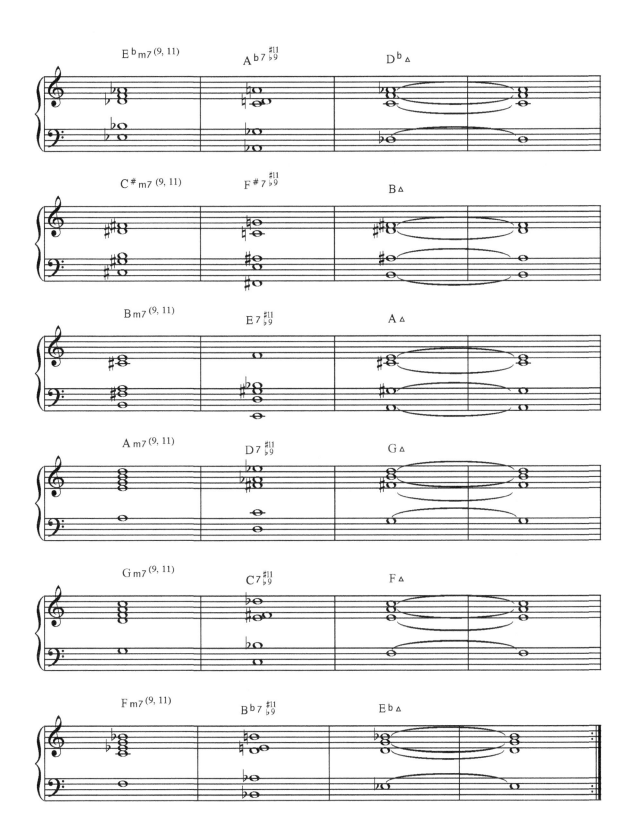

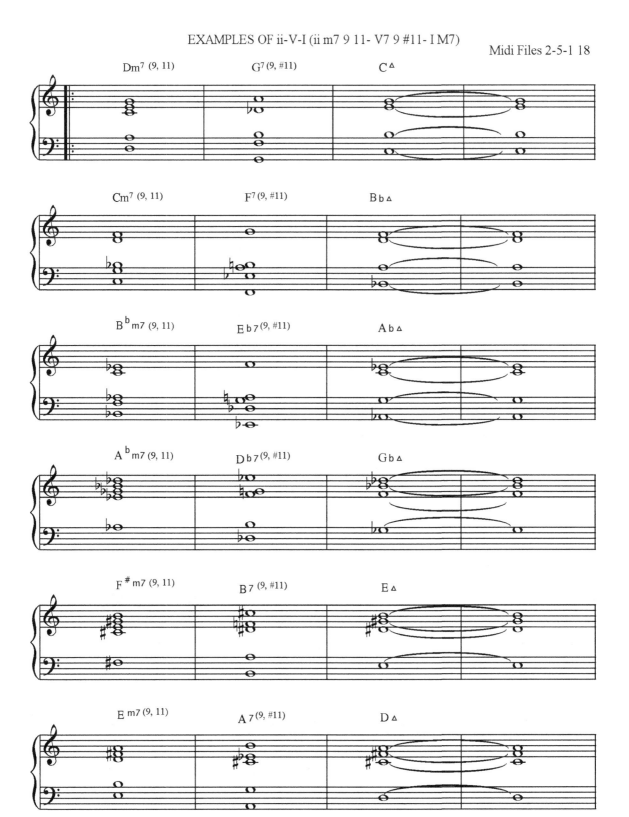

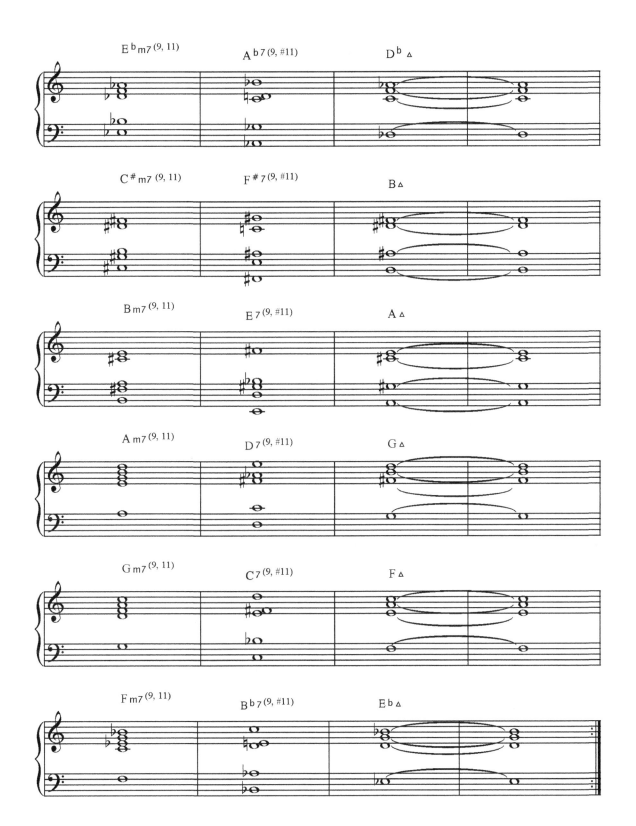

93

EXAMPLES OF ii-V-I (ii m7 9 11- V7 #9 #11- I M7)

Midi Files 2-5-1 19

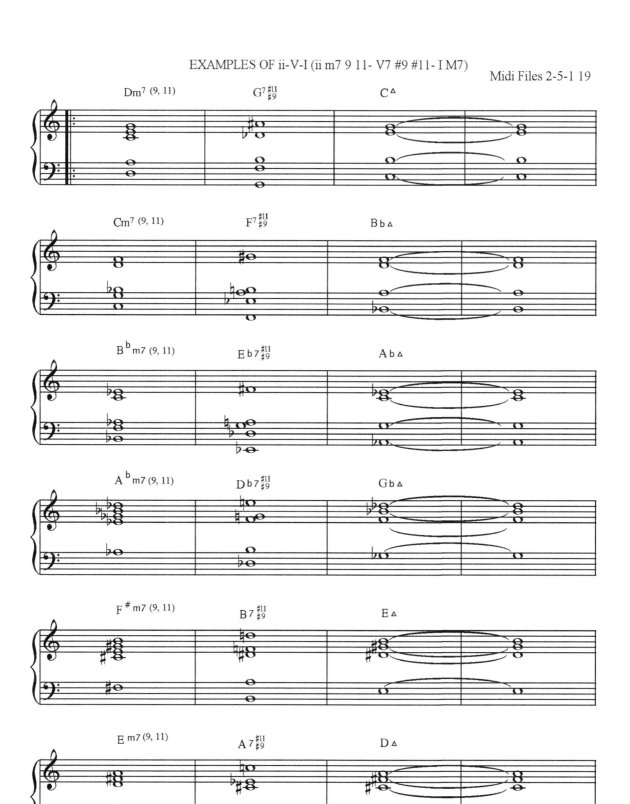

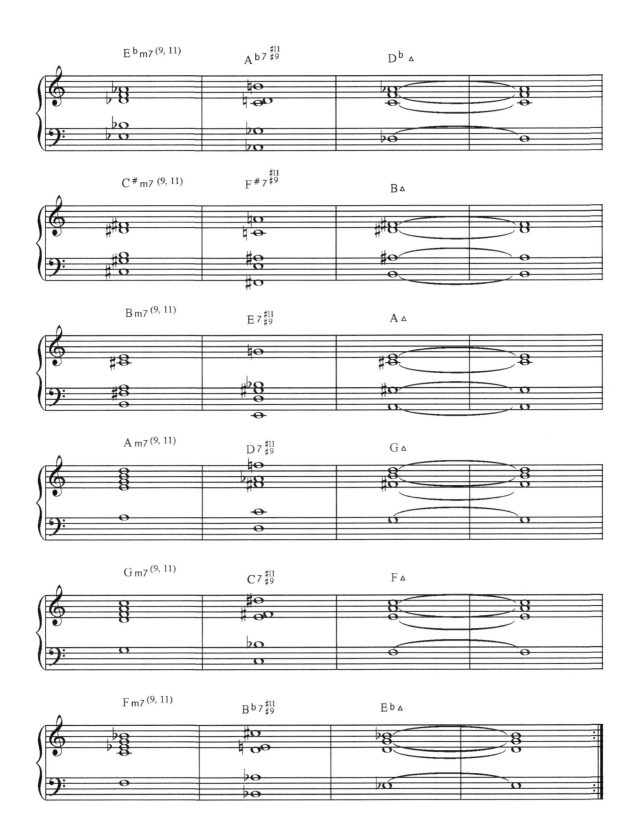

EXAMPLES OF ii-V-I (i m7 9- V 7 b9 #11 13- I M7)

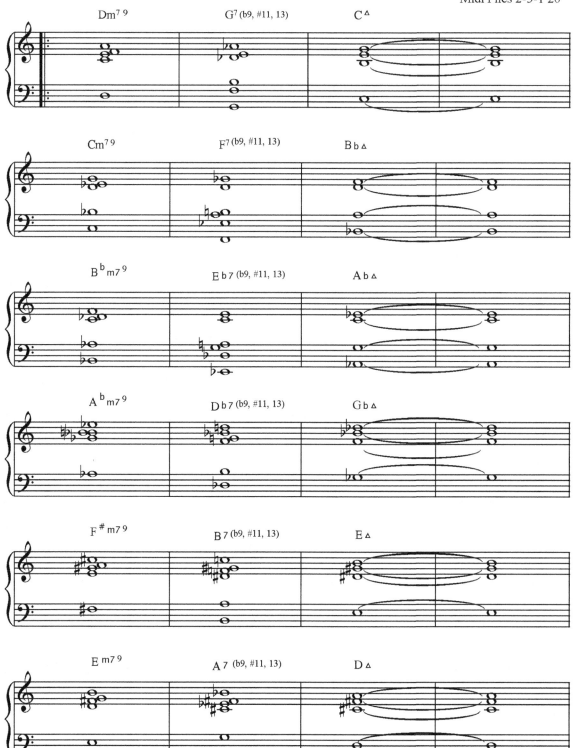

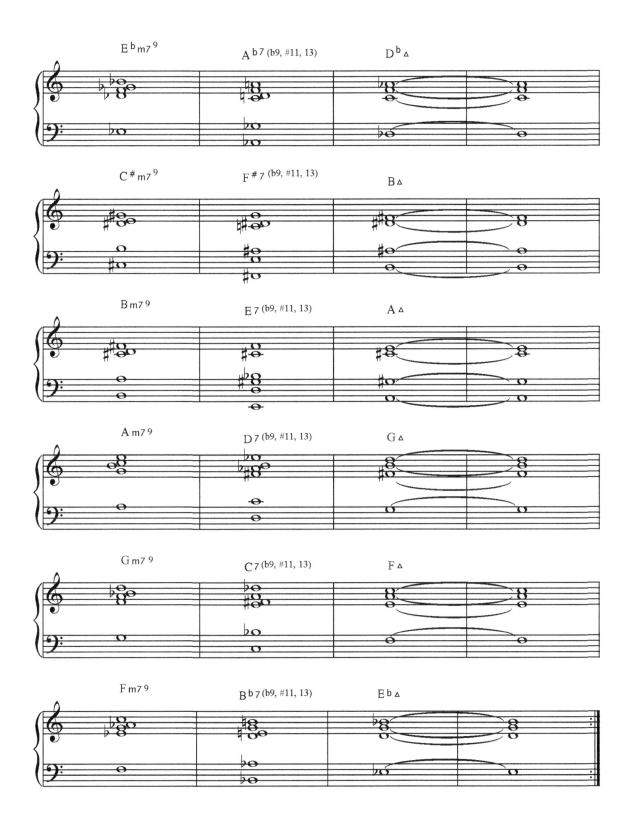

EXAMPLES OF ii-V-I (i m7 9- V7 9 #11 13- I M7)

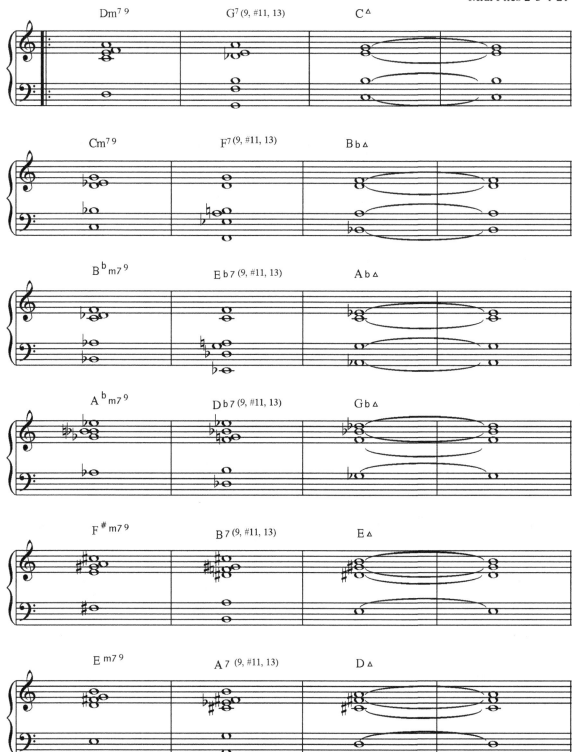

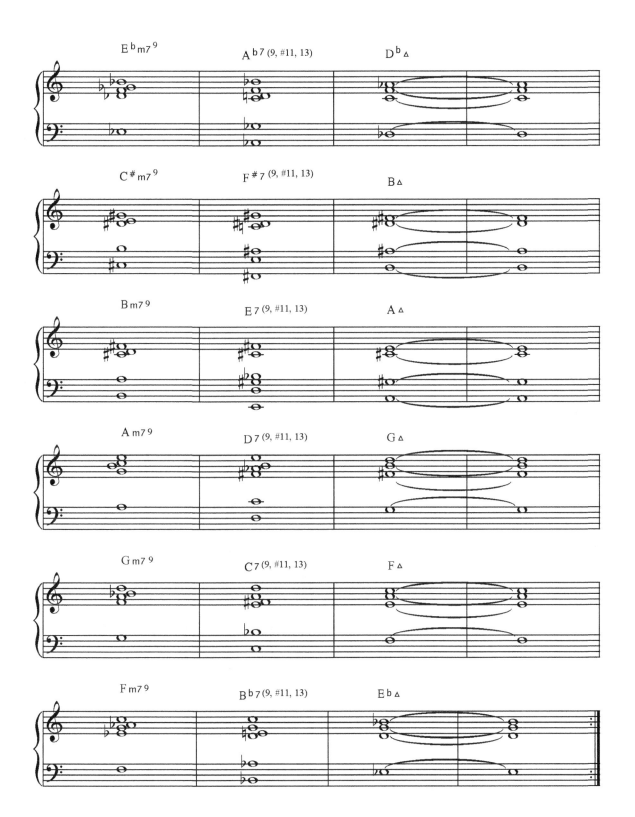

EXAMPLES OF ii-V-I (i m7 9- V7 #9 #11 13- I M7)

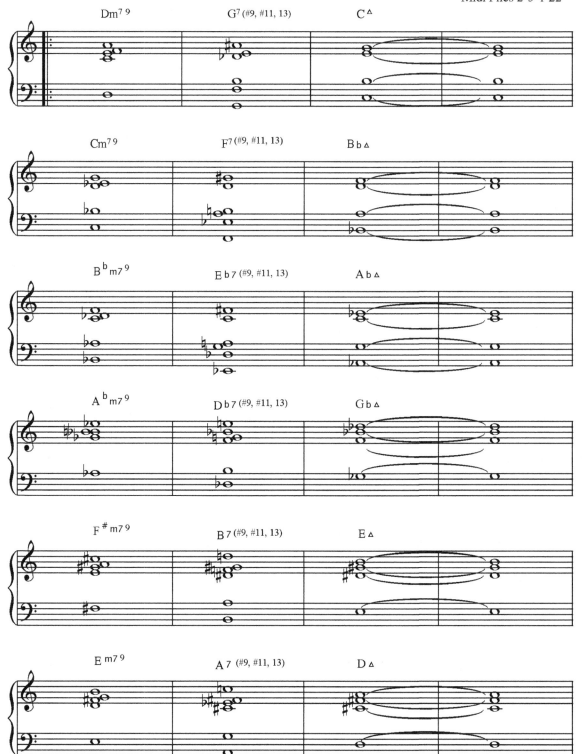

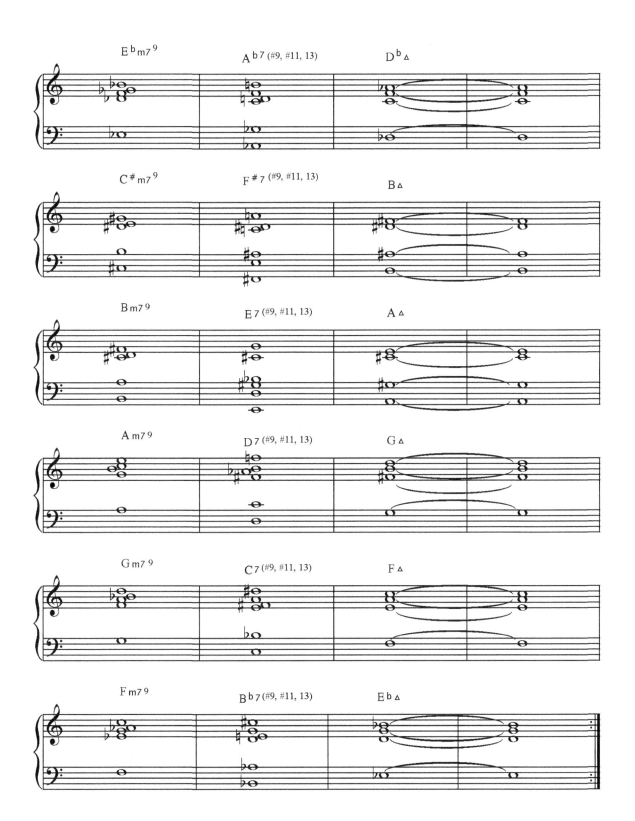

EXAMPLES OF ii-V-I (ii m7 9 11- V7 b9 #11 13- I M7)

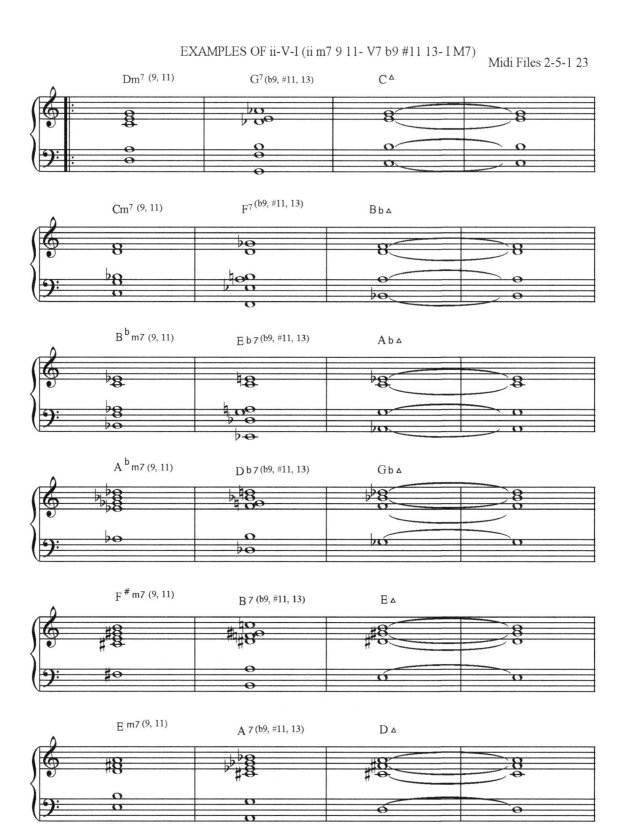

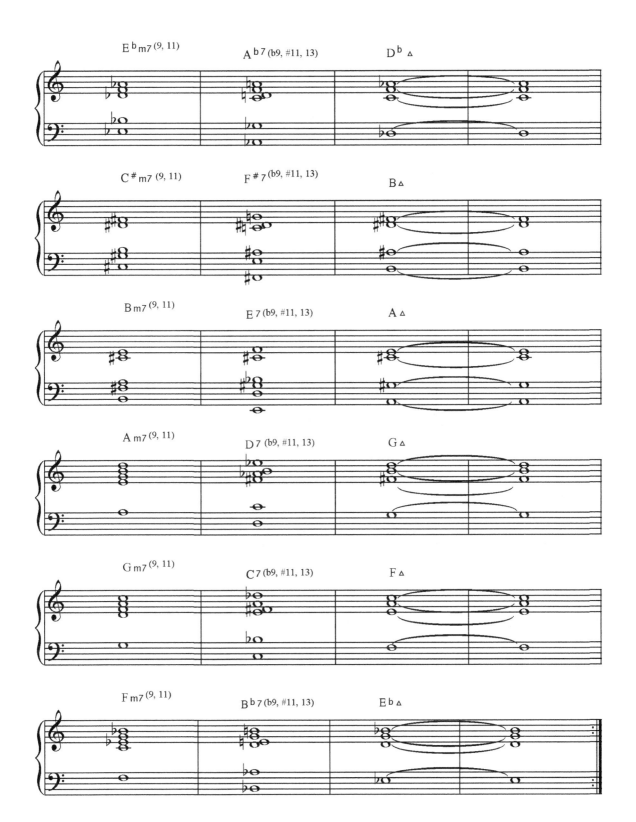

EXAMPLES OF ii-V-I (ii m7 9 11- V7 9 #11 13- I M7)

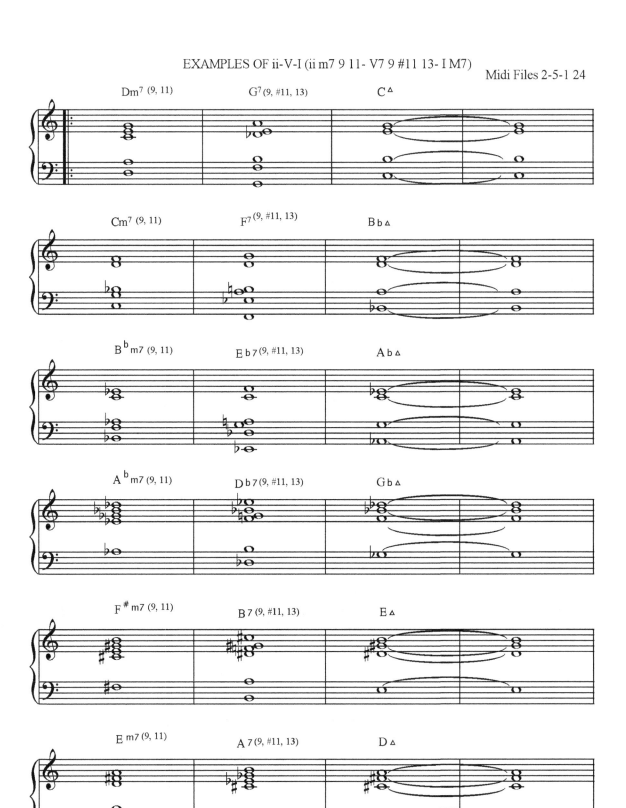

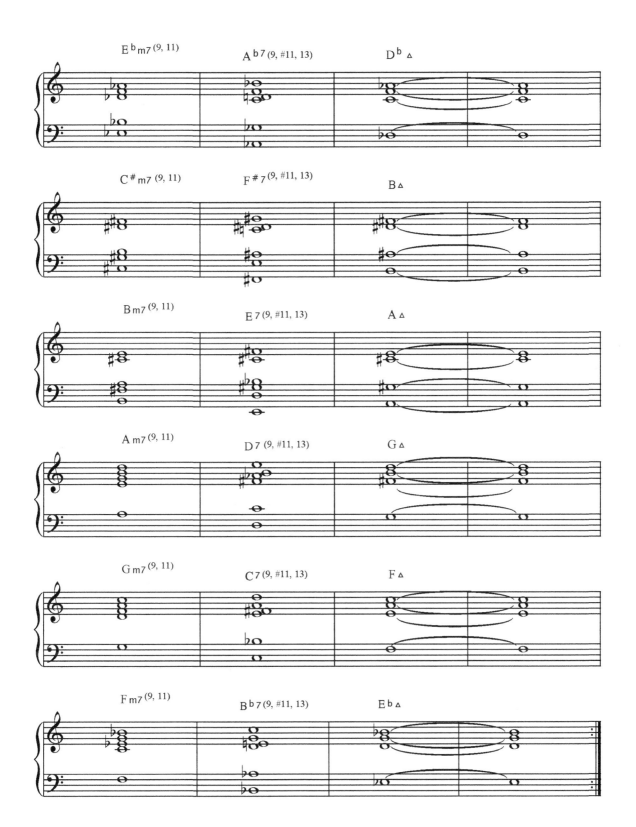

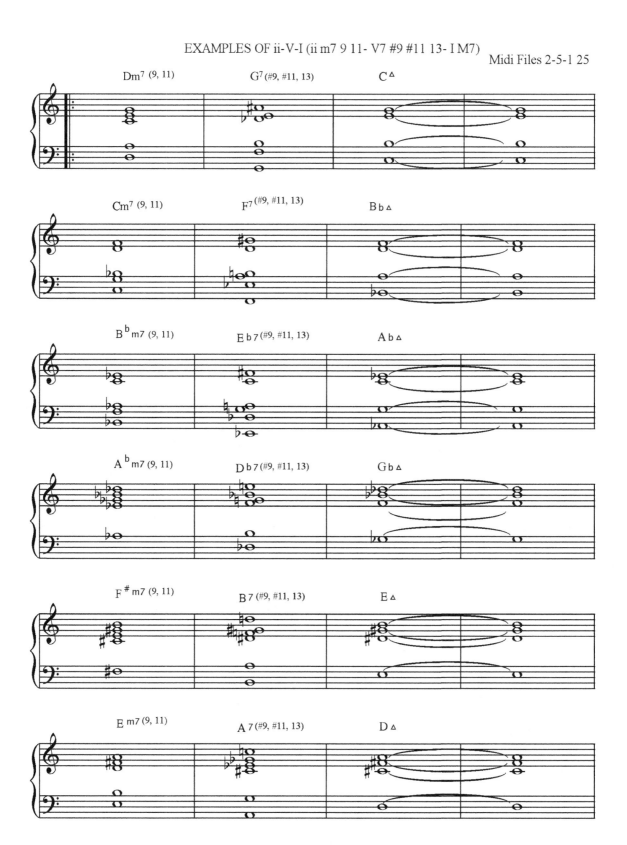

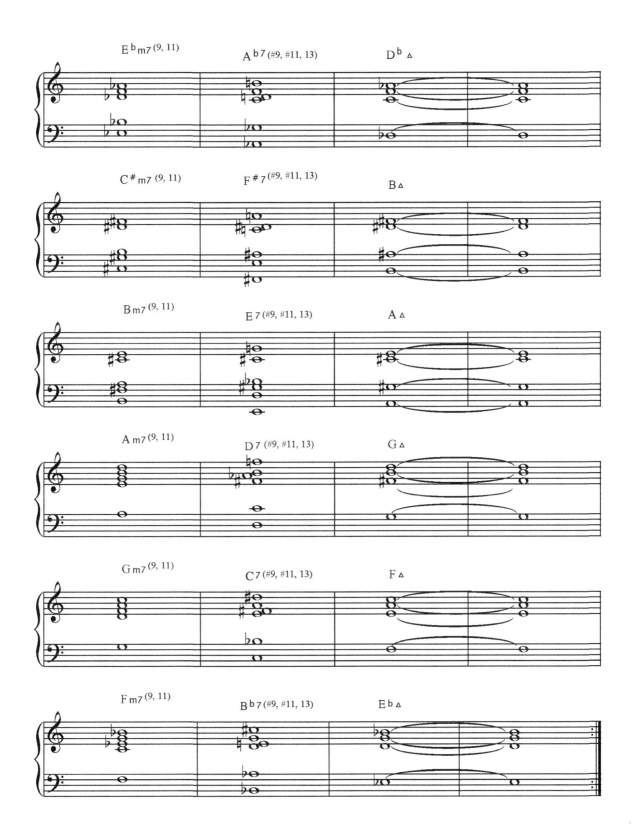

EXAMPLES OF ii-V-I (ii m7 9 11 13- V7 b9 #11 13- I M7)

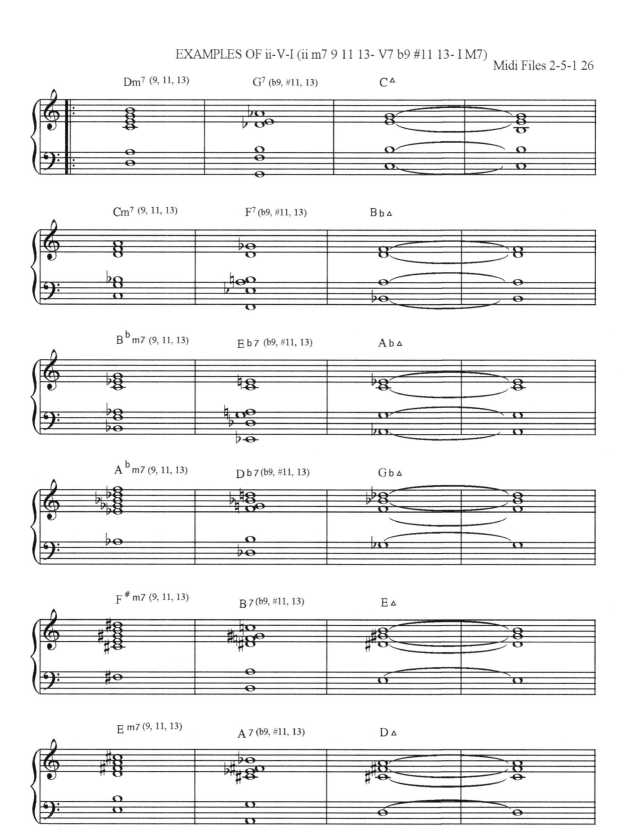

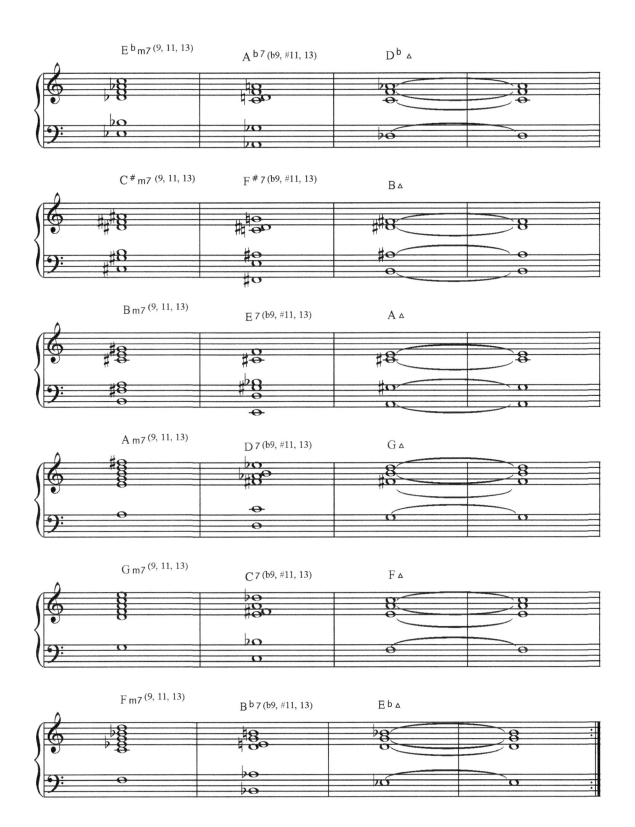

109

EXAMPLES OF ii-V-I (ii m7 9 11 13- V7 b9 #11 13- I M7)

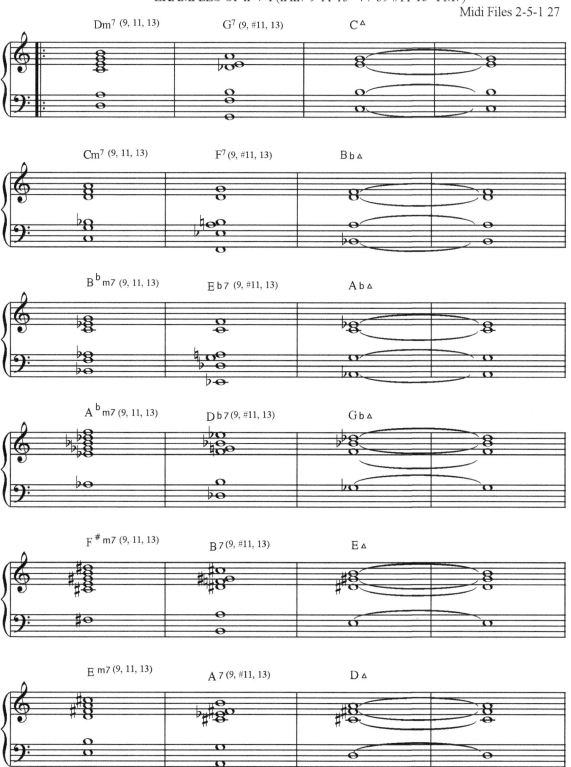

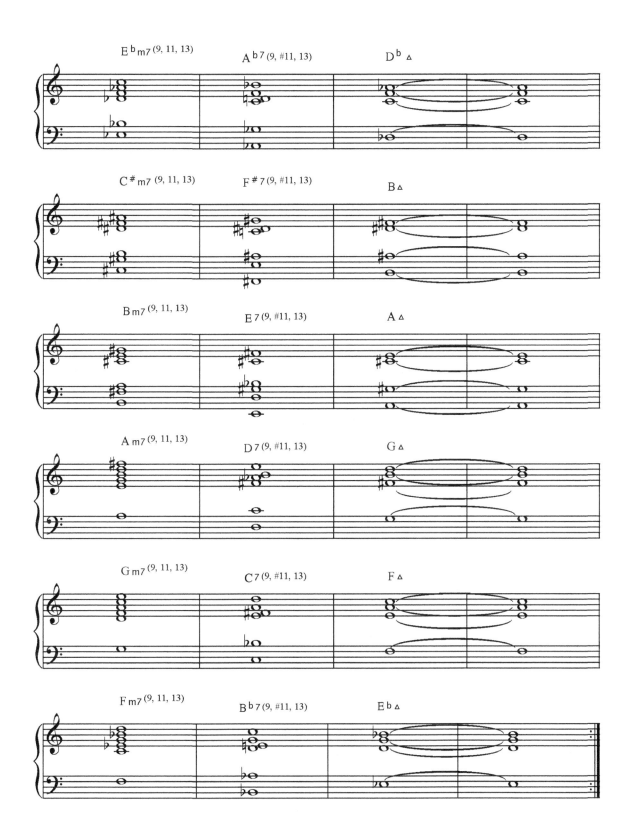

111

EXAMPLES OF ii-V-I (ii m7 9 11 13- V7 #9 #11 13- I M7)

Midi Files 2-5-1 28

Dm⁷ (9, 11, 13)　　　G⁷ (#9, #11, 13)　　　Cᐃ

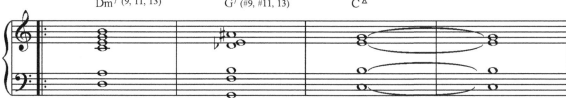

Cm⁷ (9, 11, 13)　　　F⁷ (#9, #11, 13)　　　Bbᐃ

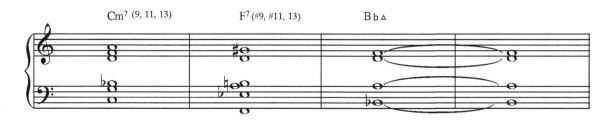

Bᵇm7 (9, 11, 13)　　　Eb7 (#9, #11, 13)　　　Abᐃ

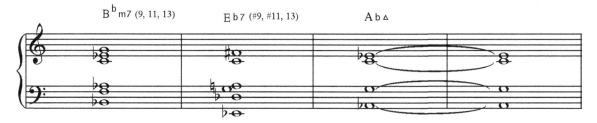

Aᵇm7 (9, 11, 13)　　　Db7 (#9, #11, 13)　　　Gbᐃ

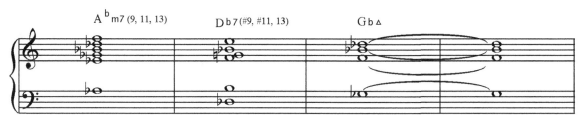

F#m7 (9, 11, 13)　　　B7 (#9, #11, 13)　　　Eᐃ

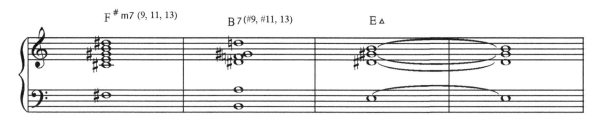

E m7 (9, 11, 13)　　　A 7 (#9, #11, 13)　　　Dᐃ

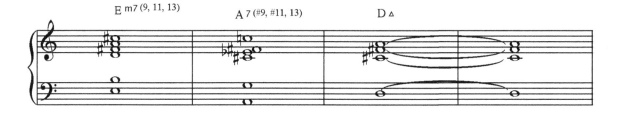

112

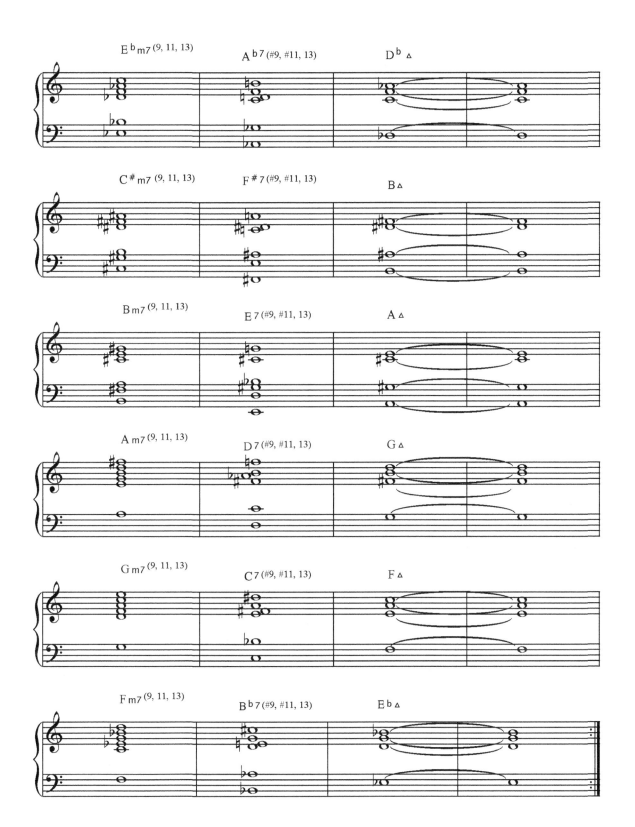

113

EXAMPLES OF ii-V-I (i m7 9- V 7 b9 #11 b13- I M7)

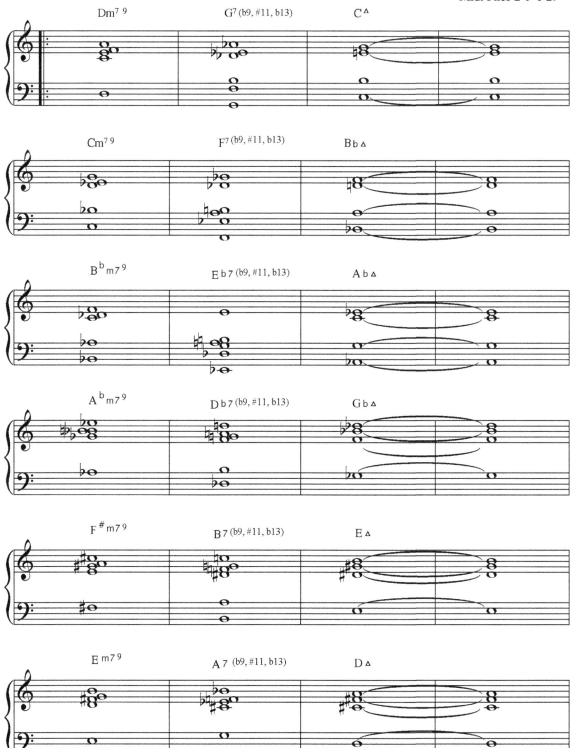

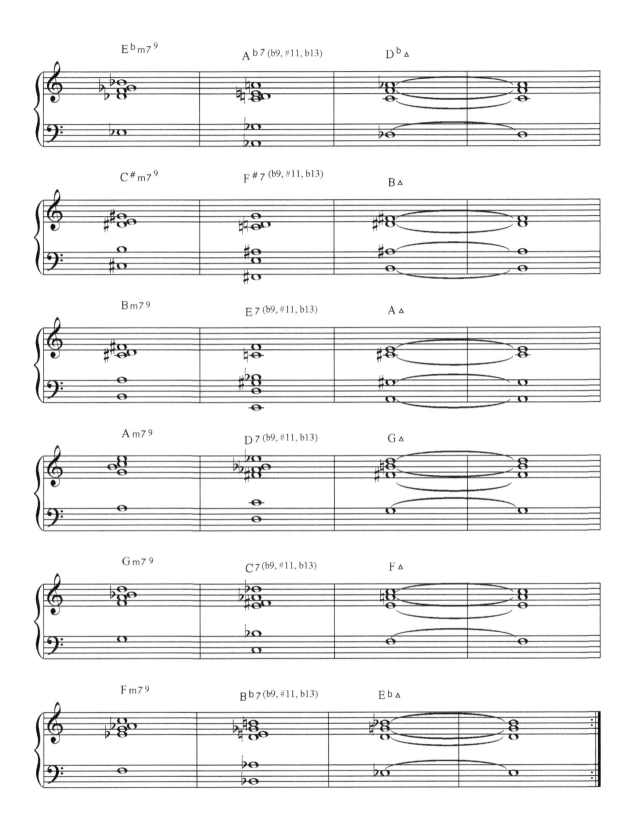

EXAMPLES OF ii-V-I (i m7 9- V7 9 #11 b13- I M7)

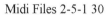Midi Files 2-5-1 30

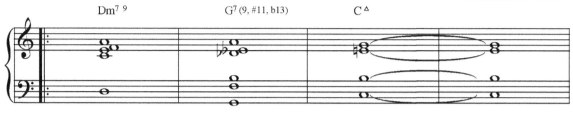

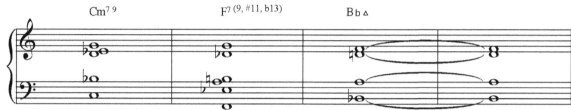

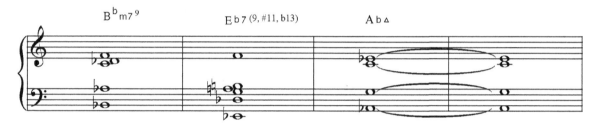

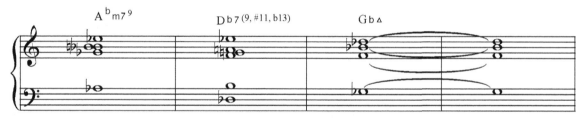

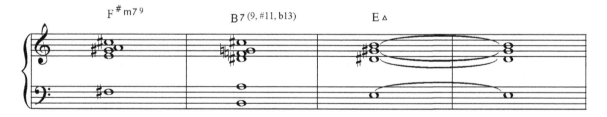

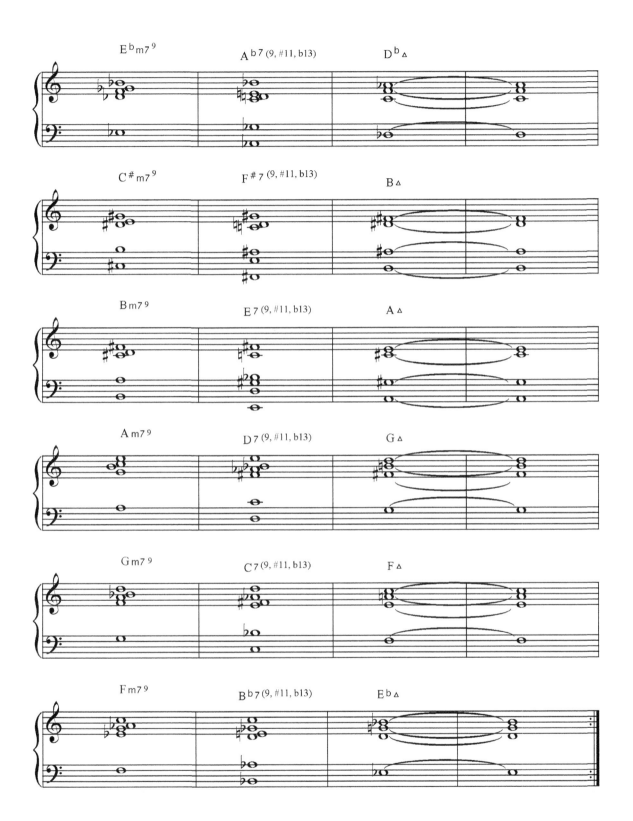

EXAMPLES OF ii-V-I (i m7 9- V7 #9 #11 b13- I M7)

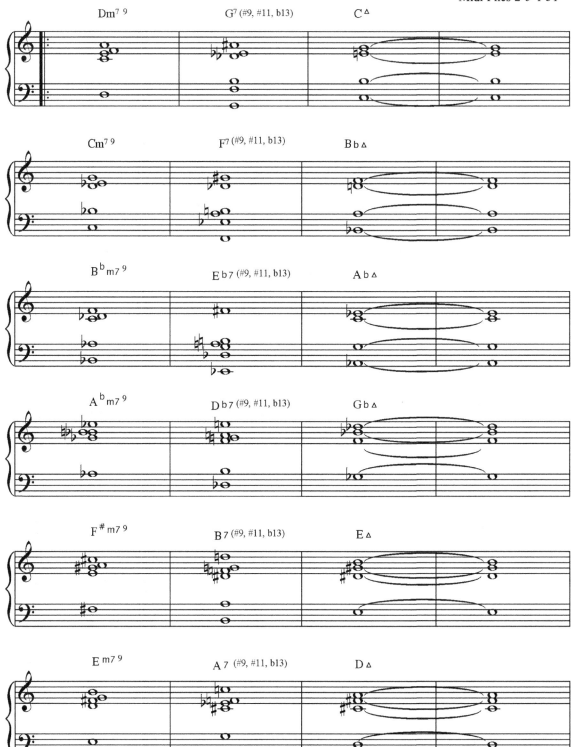

118

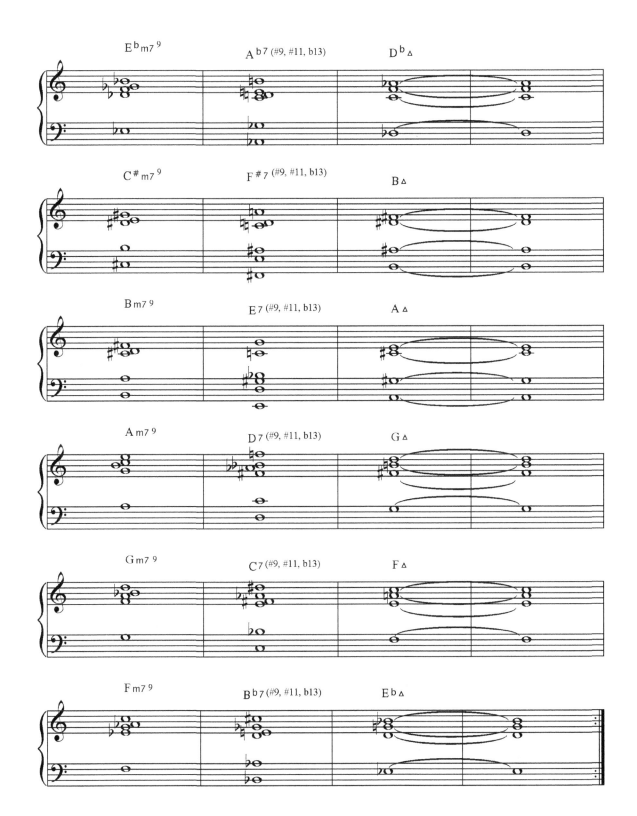

EXAMPLES OF ii-V-I (ii m7 9 11- V7 b9 #11 b13- I M7)

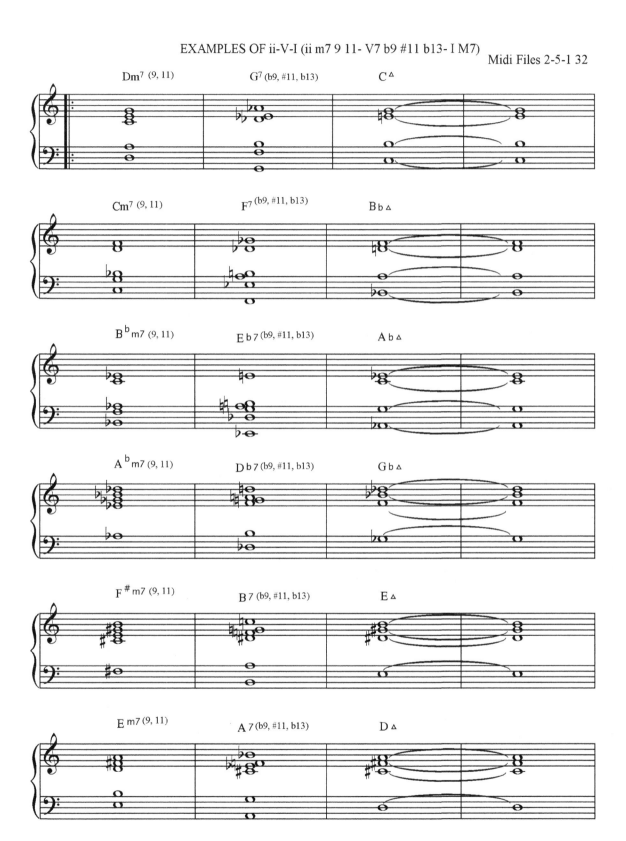

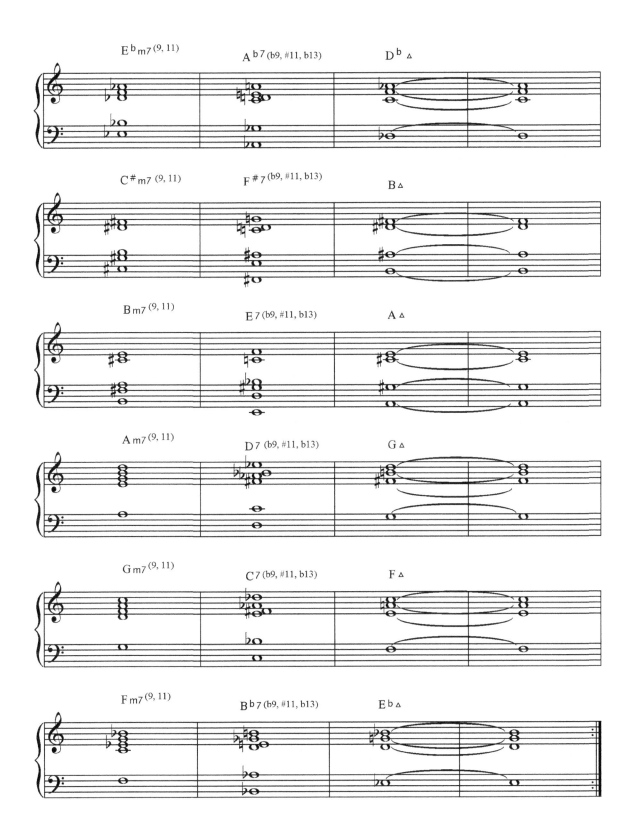

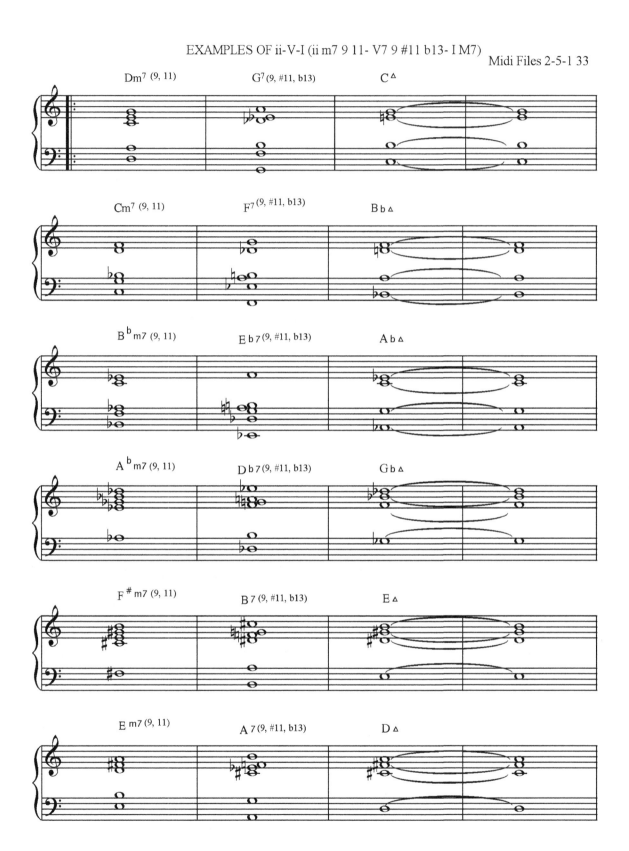

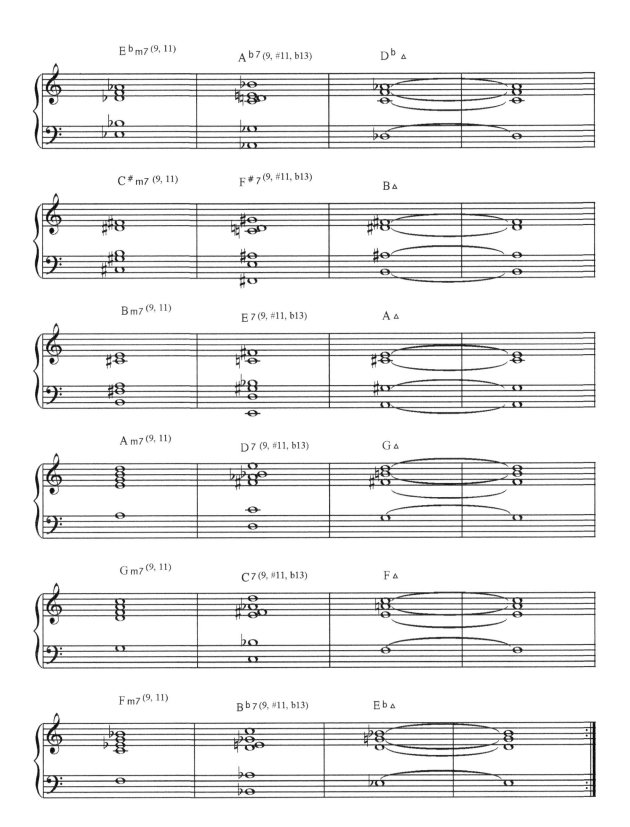

123

EXAMPLES OF ii-V-I (ii m7 9 11- V7 #9 #11 b13- I M7)

Midi Files 2-5-1 34

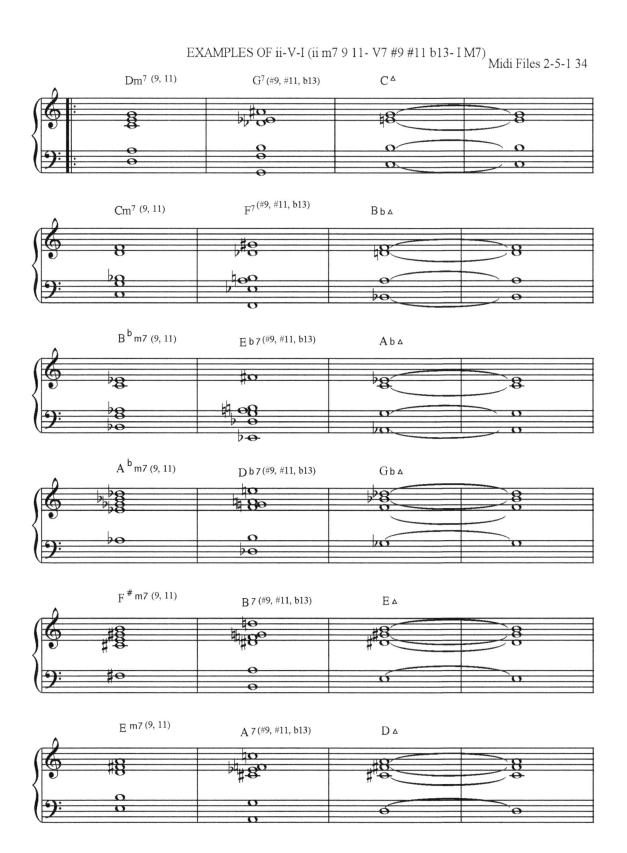

124

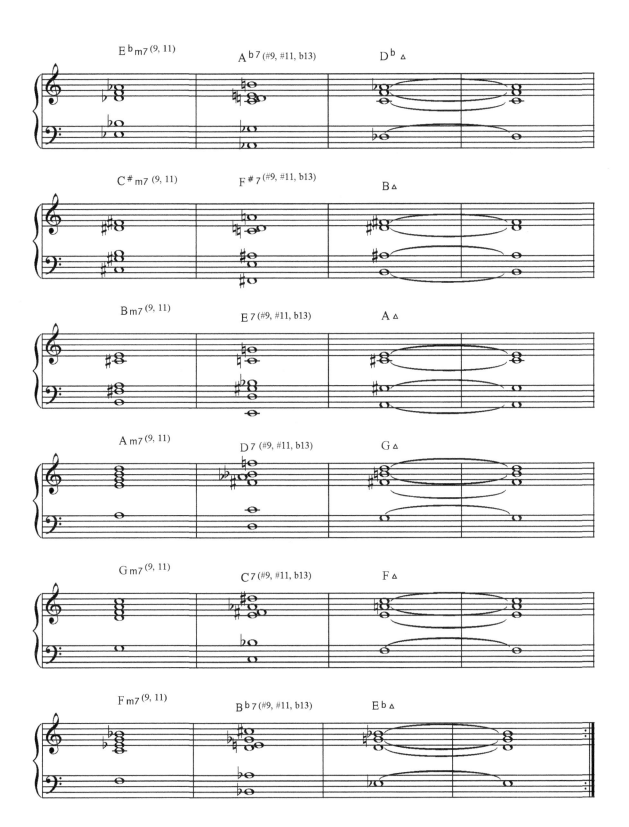

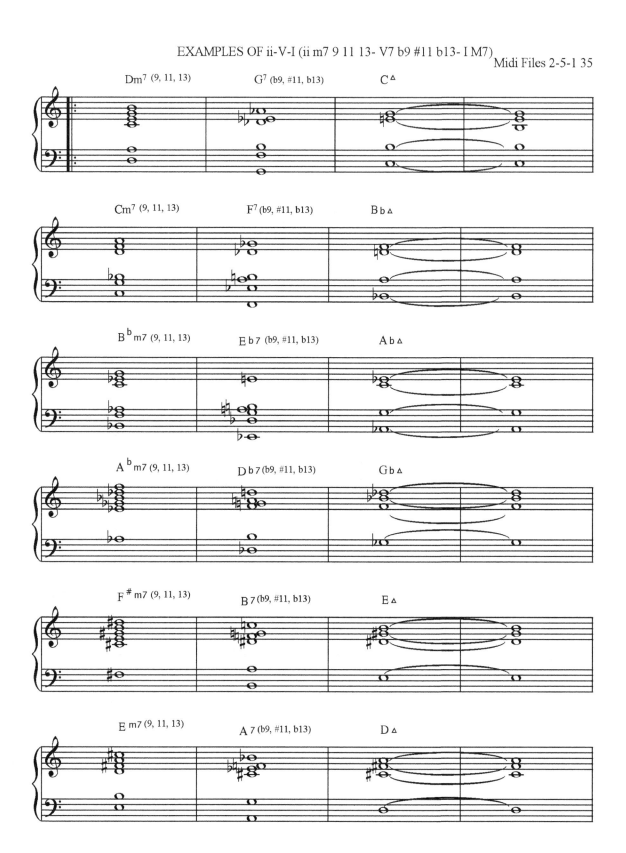

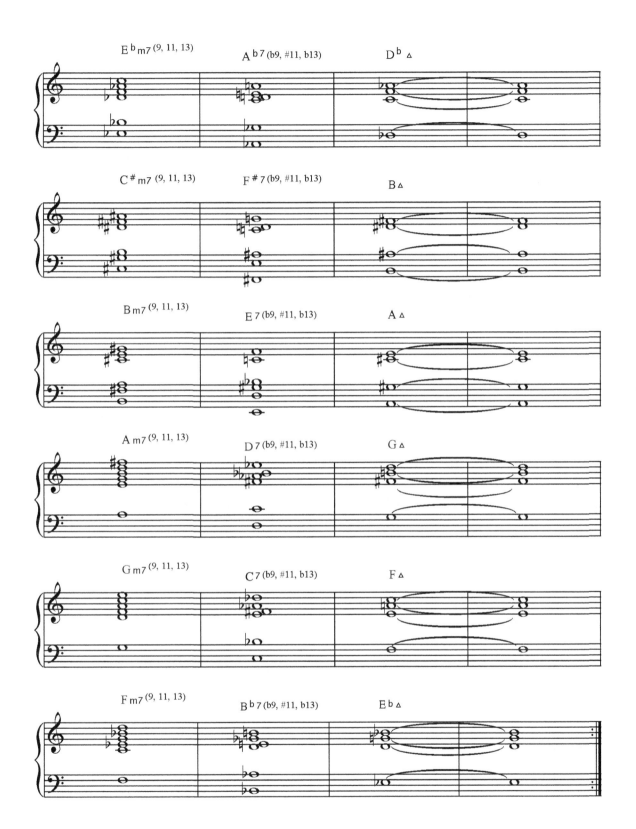

EXAMPLES OF ii-V-I (ii m7 9 11 13- V7 b9 #11 b13- I M7)

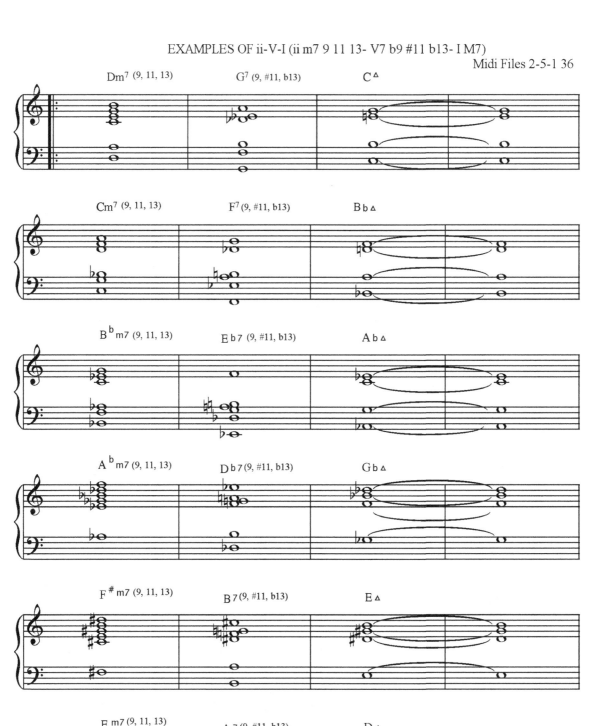

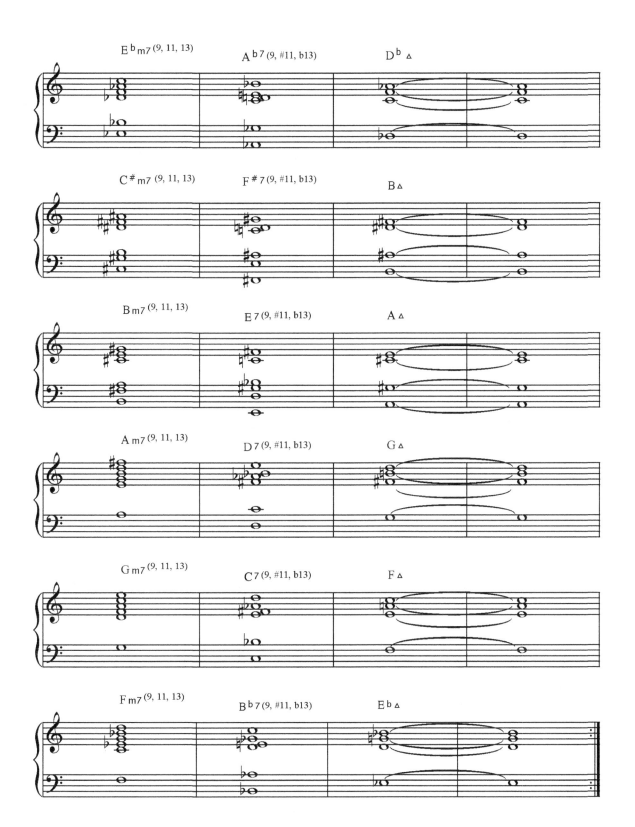

129

EXAMPLES OF ii-V-I (ii m7 9 11 13- V7 #9 #11 b13- I M7)

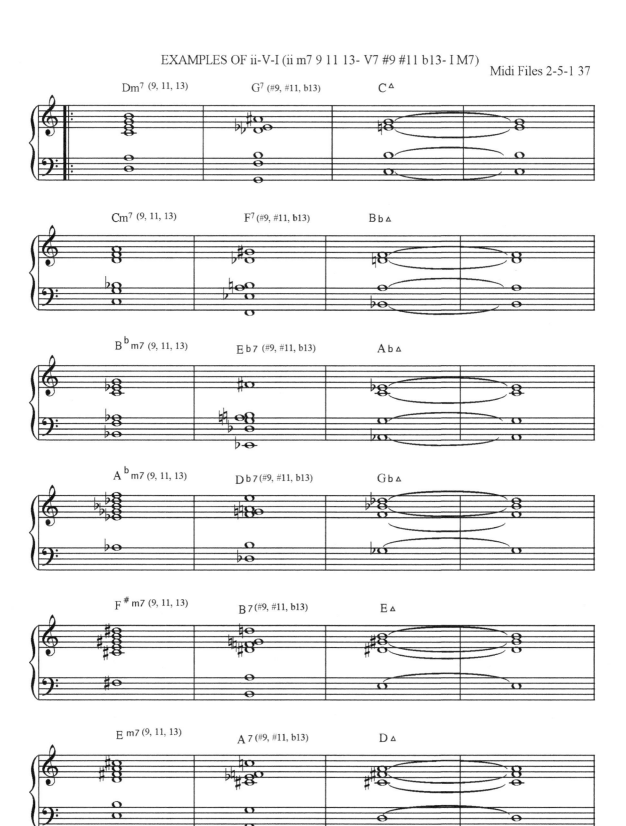

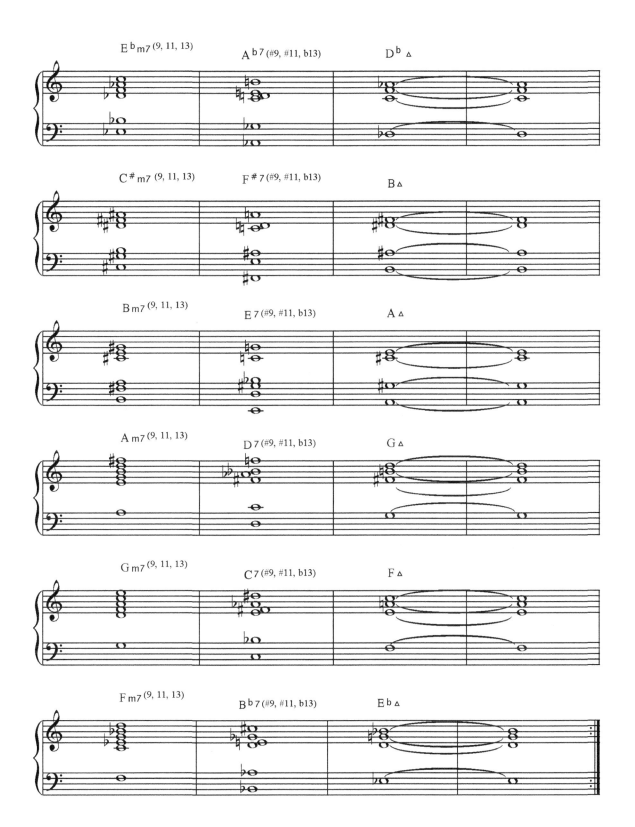

EXAMPLES OF ii-V-I (i m7 9- V Phrygian- I M7 9)

Dm⁷ ⁹   G Phr   C△⁹

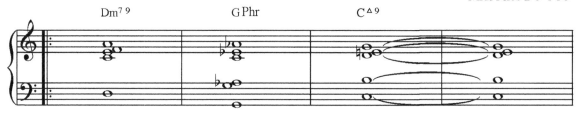

Cm⁷⁹   F Phr   Bb△⁹

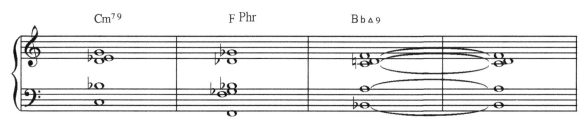

B♭m⁷⁹   E♭ Phr   Ab△⁹

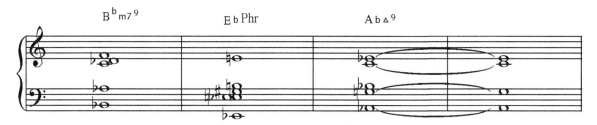

A♭m⁷⁹   D♭ Phr   Gb△⁹

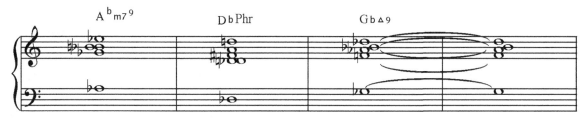

F♯m⁷⁹   B Phr   E△⁹

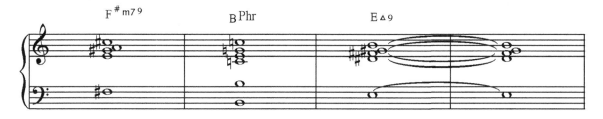

Em⁷⁹   A Phr   D△⁹

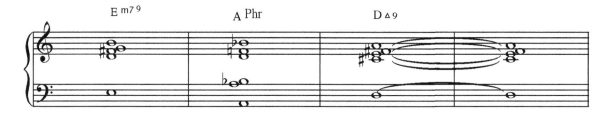

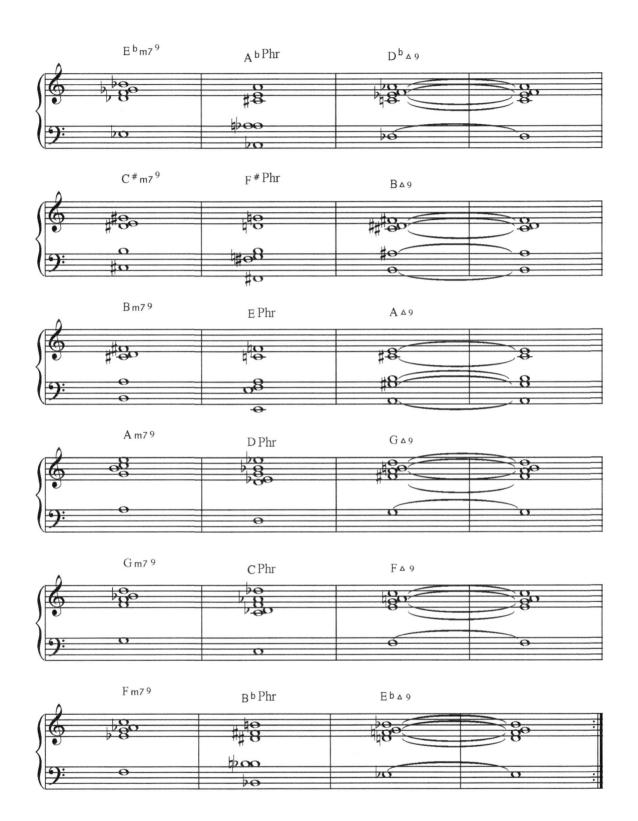

133

EXAMPLES OF ii-V-I (i m7 9 11- V Phrygian- I M7 9 #11)

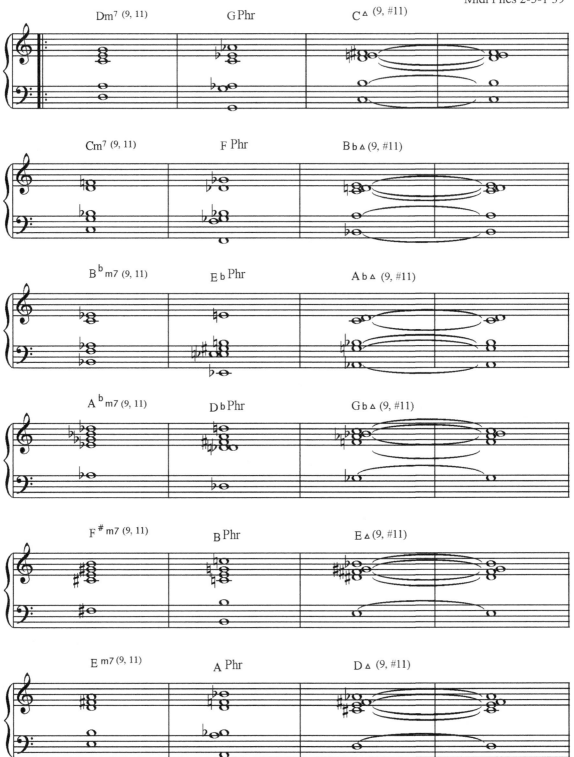

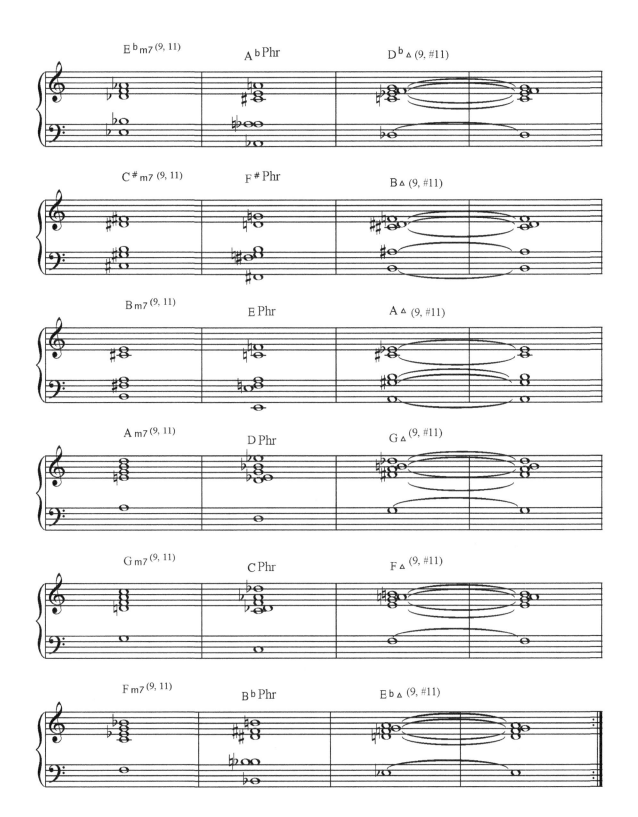

EXAMPLES OF ii-V-I (ii m7 9 11 13- V Phrygian - I M7 9 #11 13)

Midi Files 2-5-1 40

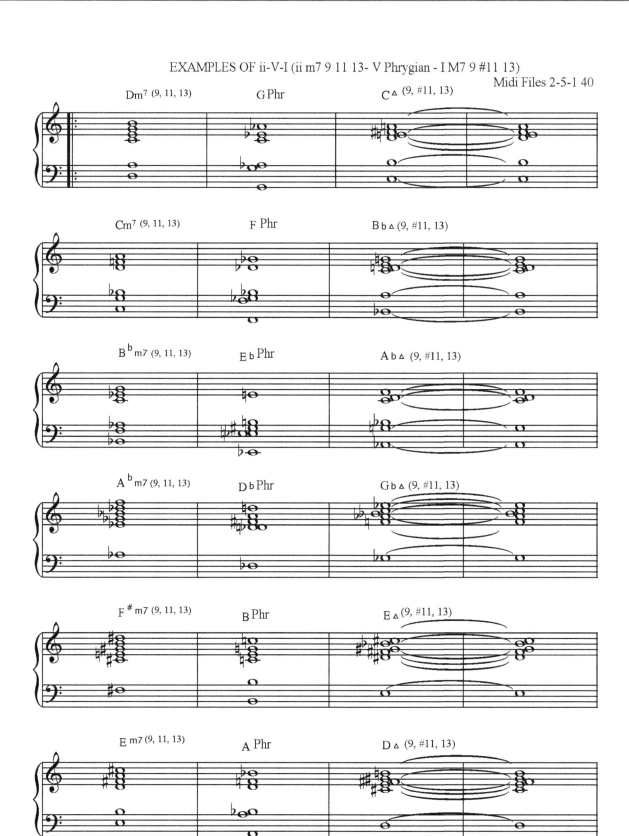

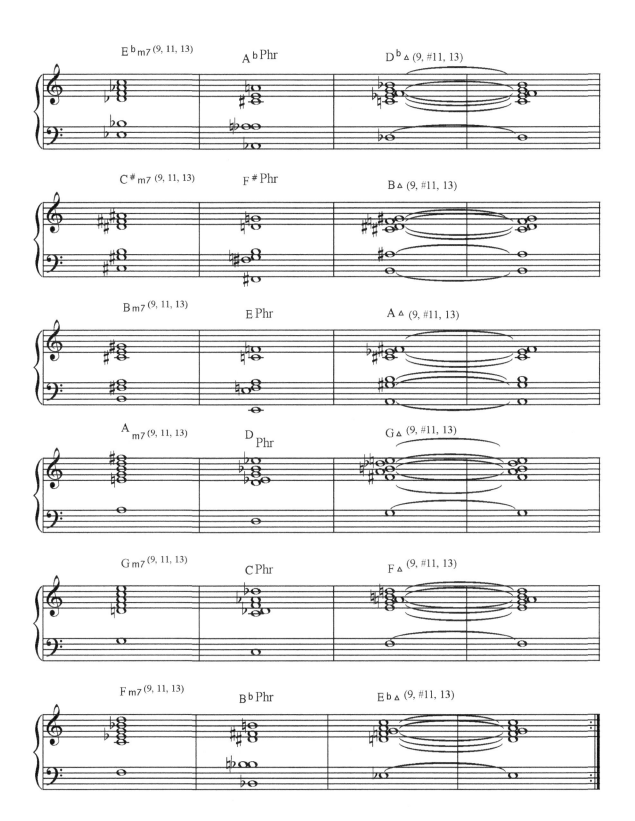

EXAMPLES OF (ii ⌀ - V7- I m7)

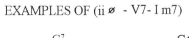

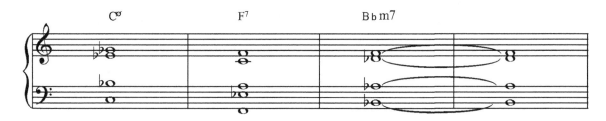

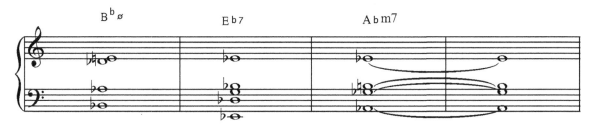

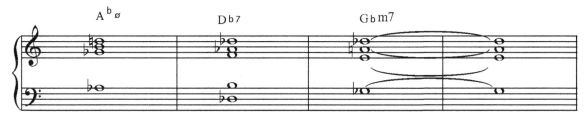

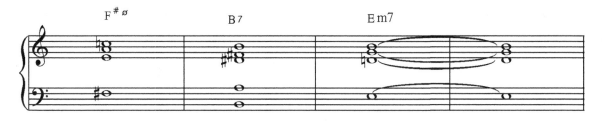

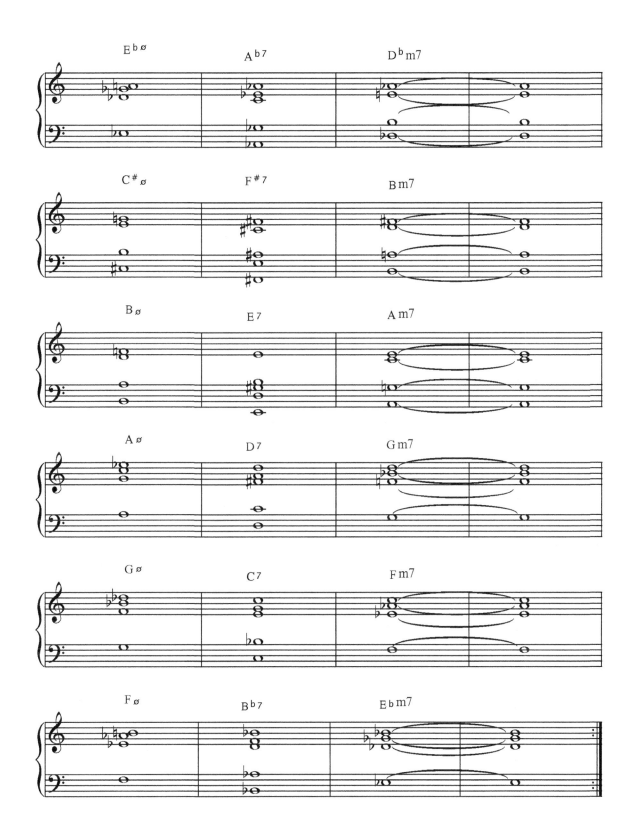

139

EXAMPLES OF (ii ø 9 - V7 b9 - I m7 9)

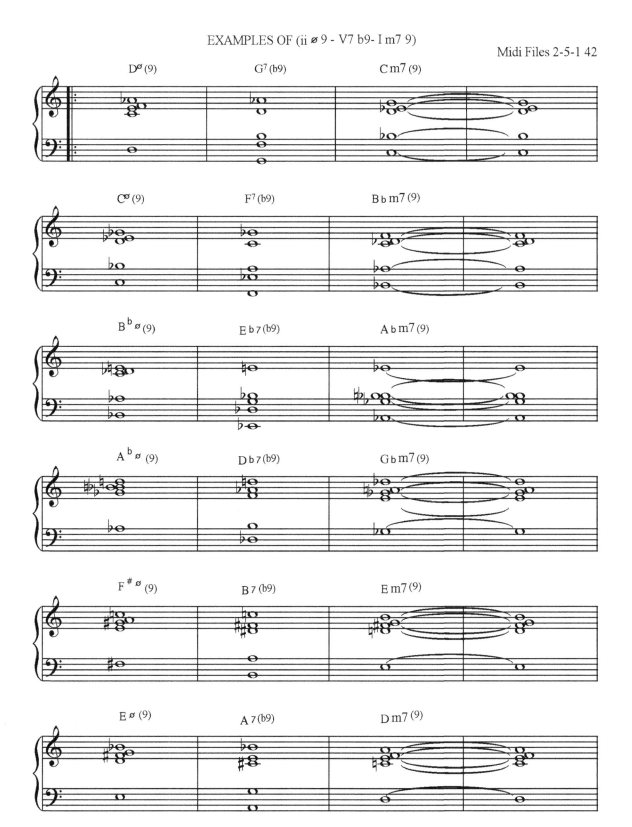

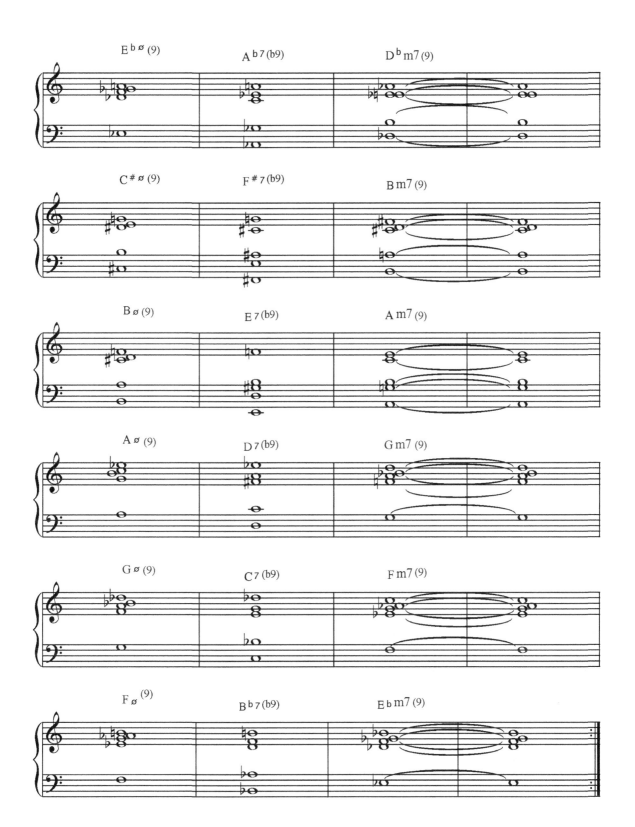

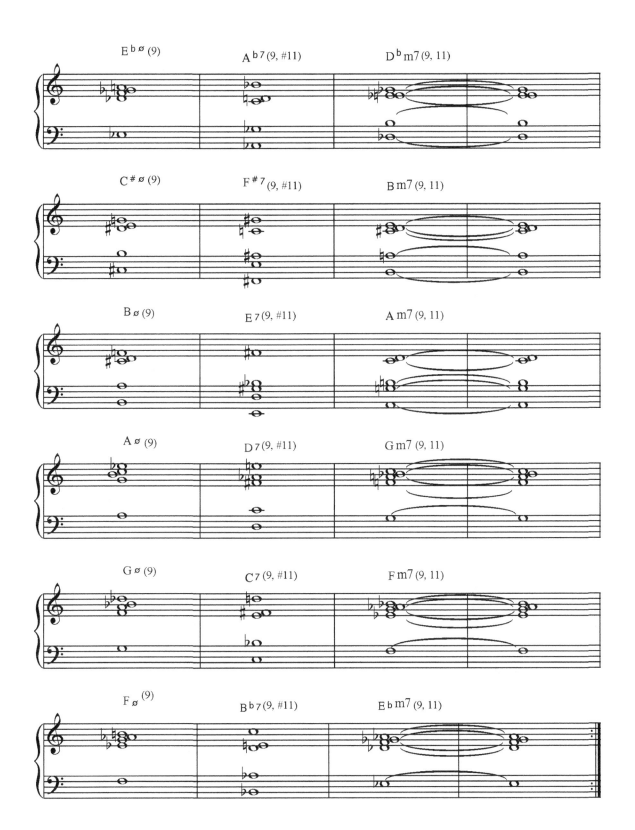

EXAMPLES OF (ii ⌀ 9 - V7 #9 #11 13 - I m7 9 11)

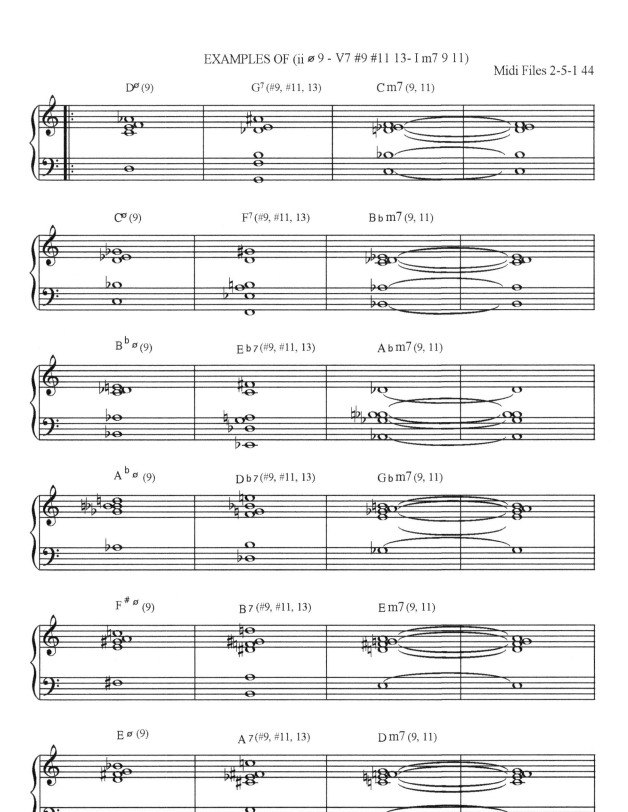

144

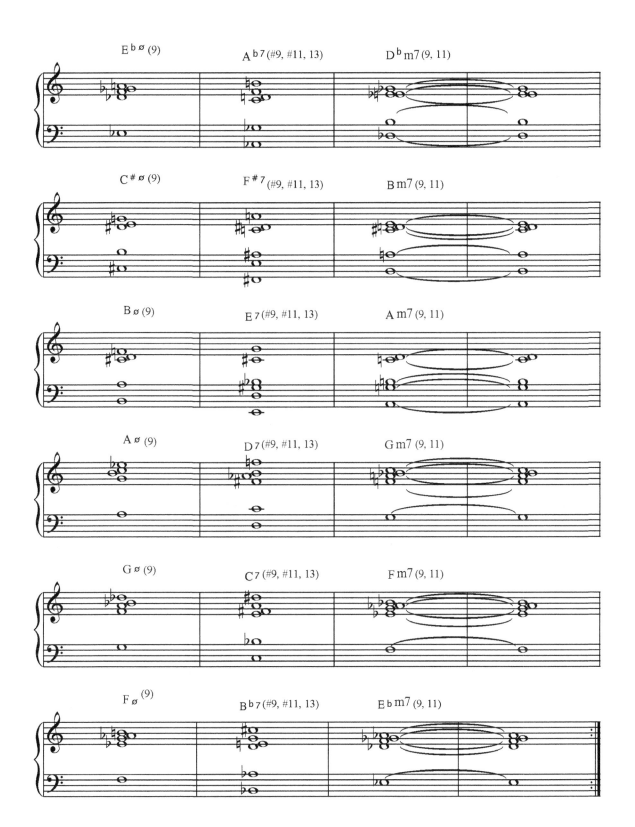

EXAMPLES OF (ii ø 9 - V7 #9 #11 b13- I m7 9 11 13)

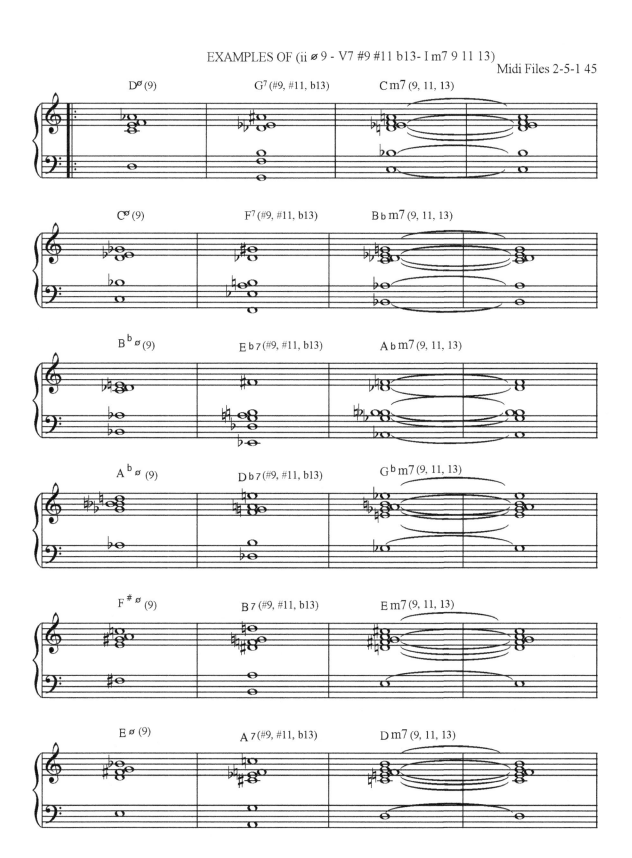

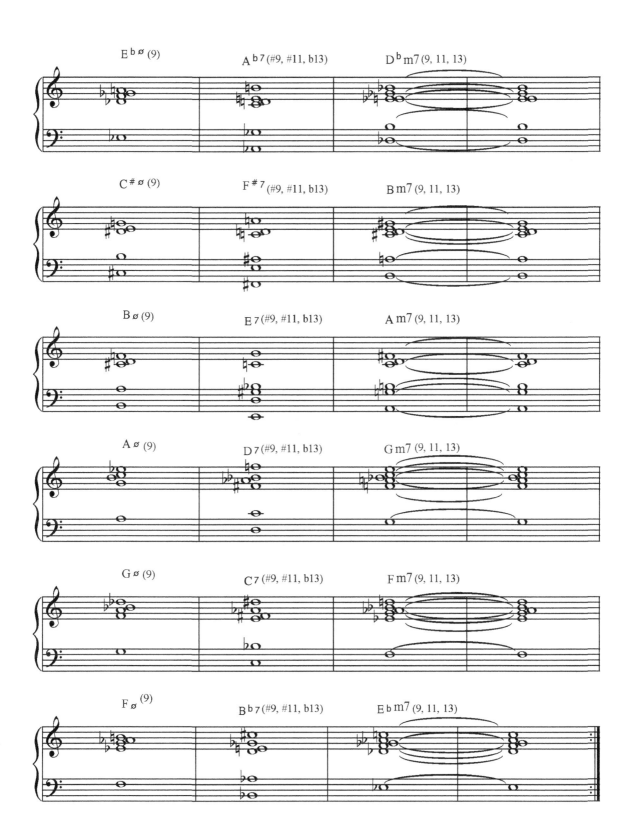

The Sus Chord/ El Acorde Suspendido

 The **Sus Chord** is a common sound in traditional & contemporary music; we might see this chord notated several ways such as; G7sus4, Gsus4, FMaj7/G or Dm7/G. The Sus Chord is very popular in Pop music.

El **acorde Suspendido** es un sonido común en la música tradicional y contemporánea; este acorde puede ser cifrado de diferentes maneras tales como; G7sus4, Gsus4, FMaj7/G o Dm7/G. Este tipo de acorde es muy popular en la música Pop.

Here we have some examples of Sus Chords/ Aquí tenemos unos ejemplos de Acordes Suspendido.

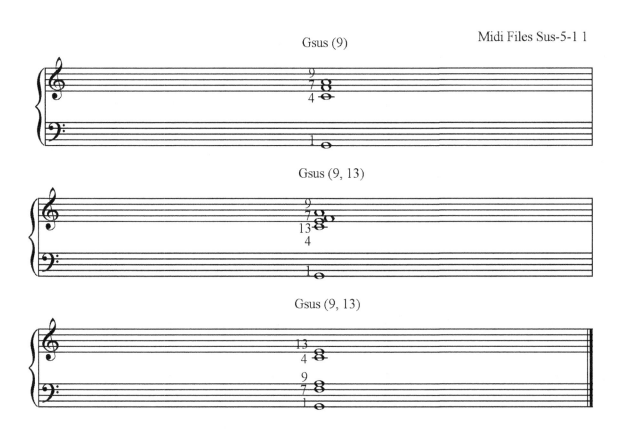

✓ In the next page, we have some examples of Sus-V-I / En la siguiente página tenemos algunos ejercicios de Sus-V-I

EXAMPLES OF Sus-V-I (Sus 9- V7- I M7)

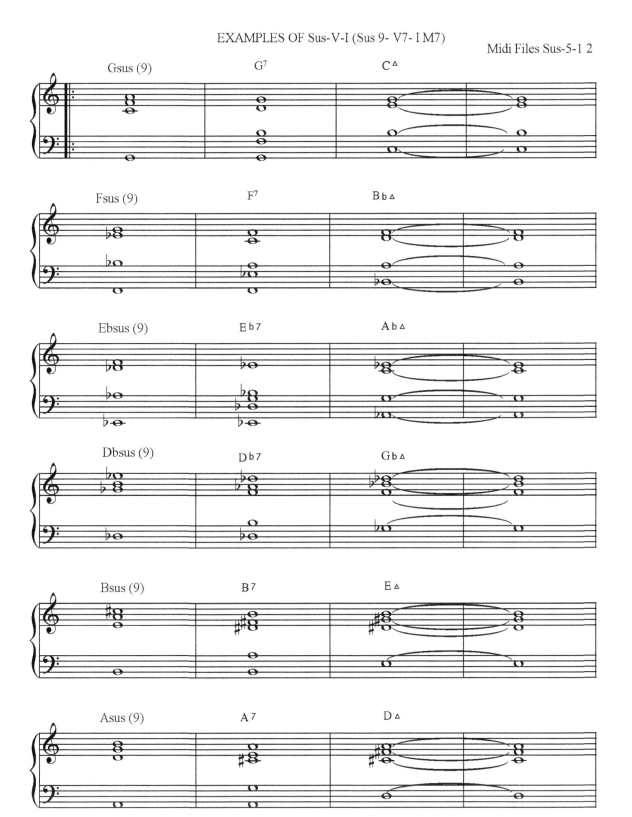

149

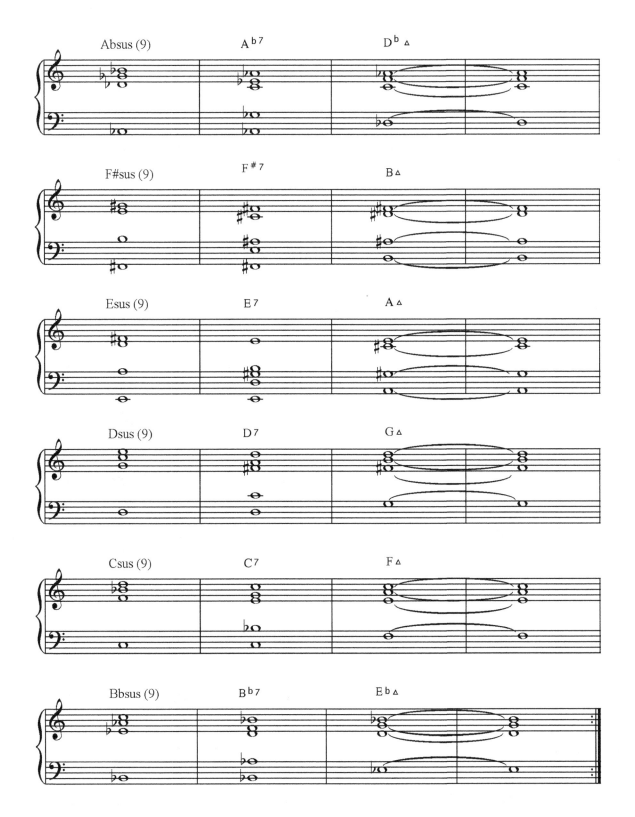

Midi Files Sus-5-1 3

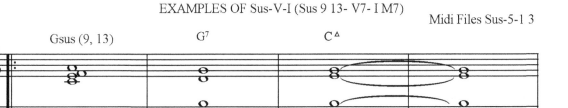

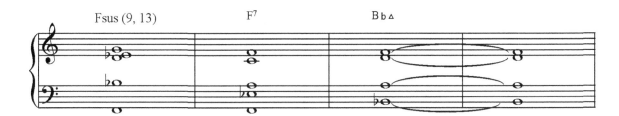

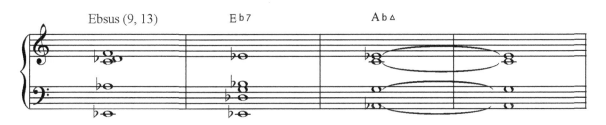

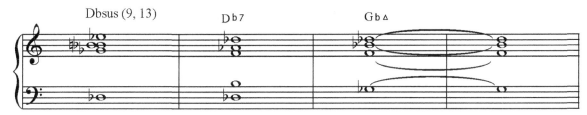

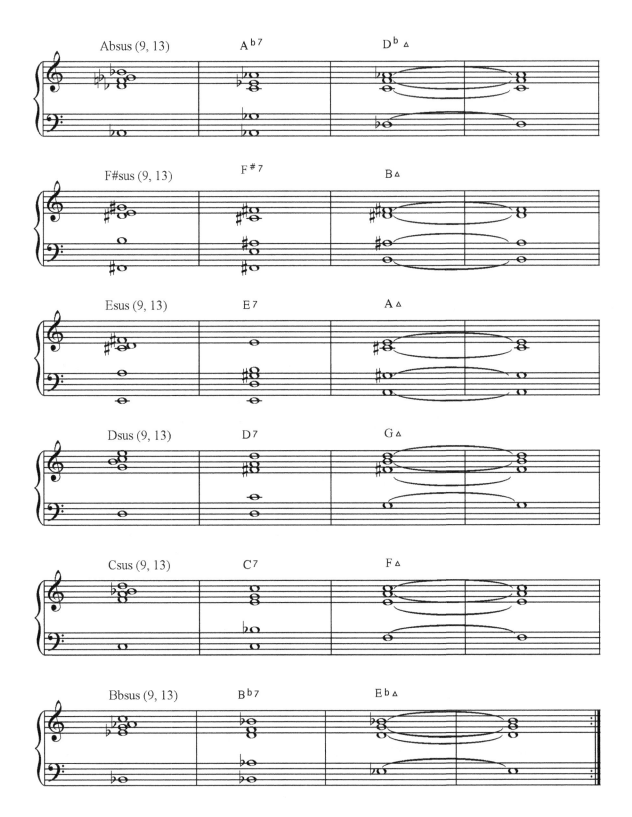

EXAMPLES OF Sus-V-I (Sus 9 11 13- V7- I M7)

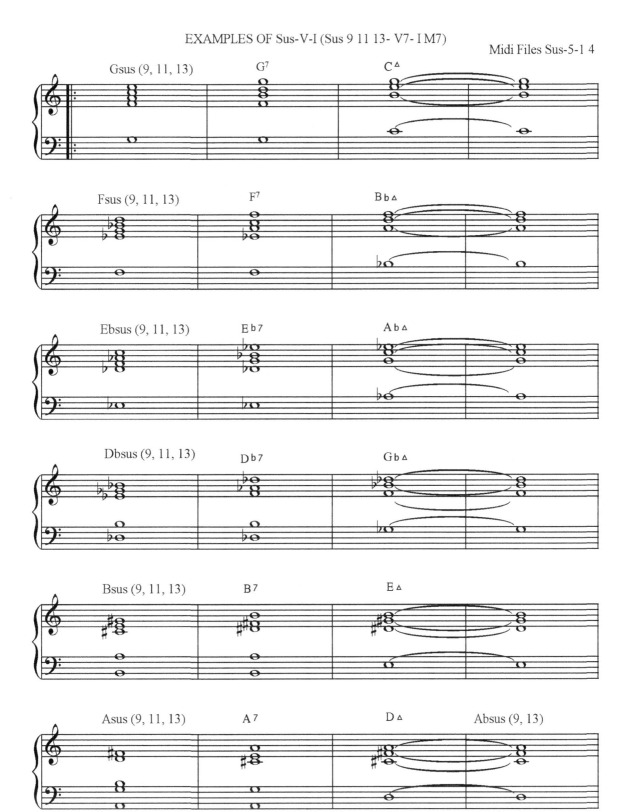

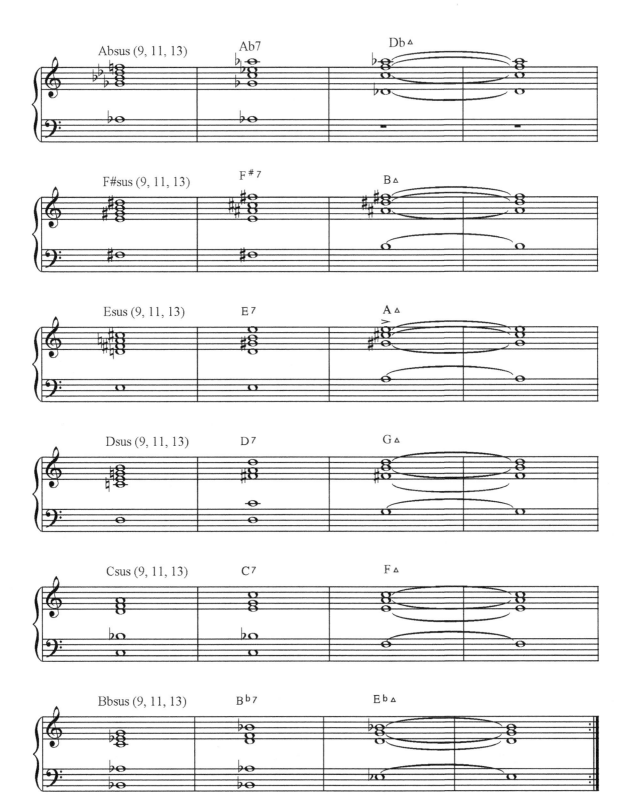

Fourth Voicing Chords

This chord is also called the "So what" chord voicing, it consist of three perfect fourth intervals followed by a major third interval.

El acorde de Cuartas también llamado el acorde "So what" consiste en tres intervalos de cuartas seguido por una tercera mayor.

"So what" is a Jazz composition based in Fourth Voicing Chords composed by Miles Davis.

"So what" es una composición de Jazz basada en acordes de Cuartas compuesta por Miles Davis.

"So What" Fourth Voicing Chord

Midi Files Fourth Chord Voicing 1

Here we have an example of a traditional Fourth voicing chord, it consist of four perfect fourth intervals.

Aquí tenemos el ejemplo de un acorde tradicional de cuartas que consiste en cuatro intervalos de cuartas.

Tradicional Fourth Voicing Chord

Midi Files Fourth Chord Voicing 2

✓ In the next page, we have some examples of Fourth Voicing Chords / En la siguiente página tenemos algunos ejercicios de acordes de Cuarta.

"So What" Fourth Voicing Chords

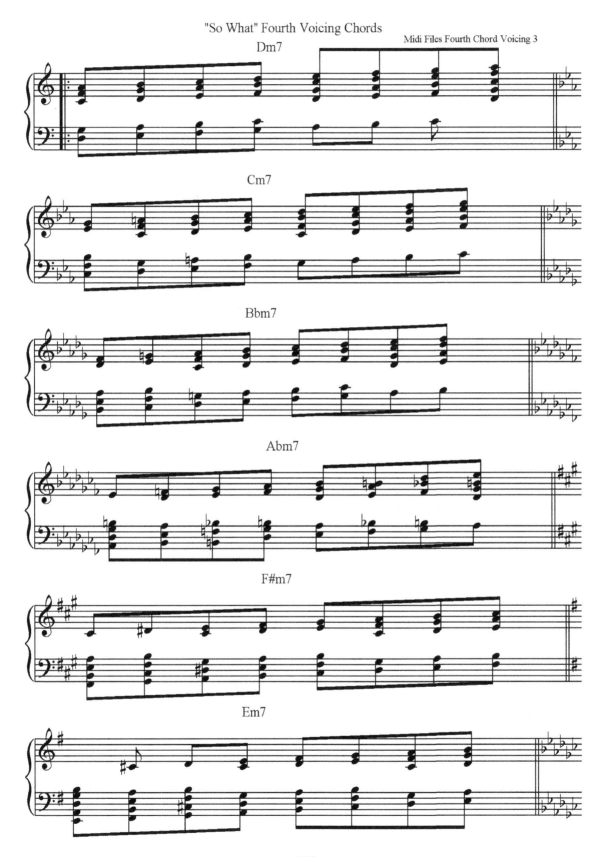

156

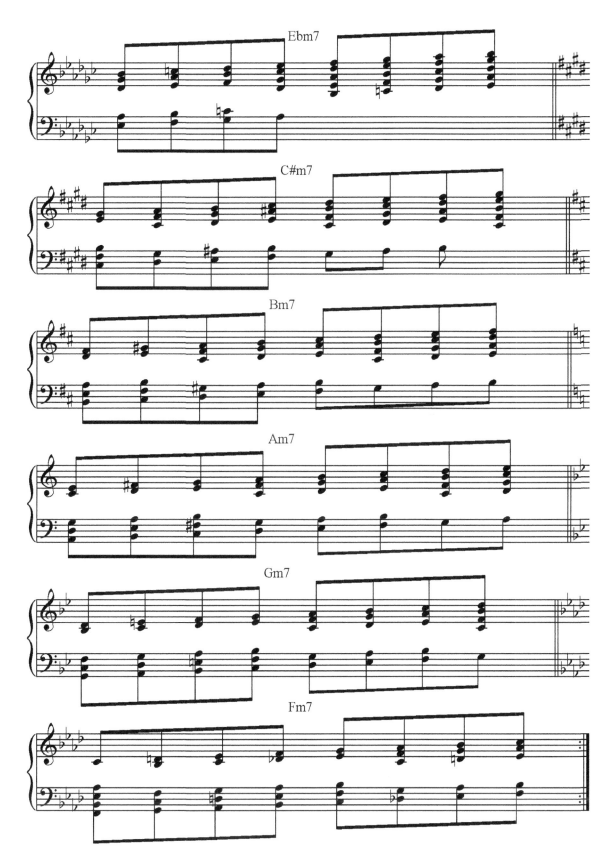

Minor 7th (b6) Chord/Aeolian Chord

- Here we have some voicing examples of a Minor7 (b6) chord.

- Aquí tenemos algunos ejemplos de un acorde Menor7 (b6).

Minor7 (b6) Chord

Midi Files Minor7 b6 1

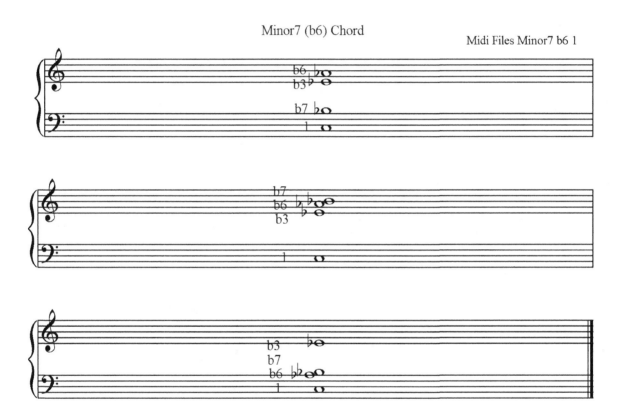

- ✓ In the next page, we have some ii-V-I examples applying the Minor7 b6.

- ✓ En la siguiente página tenemos algunos ejercicios de ii-V-I donde vamos a aplicar el acorde Menor7 b6.

EXAMPLES OF ii-V-I (ii m7 b6- V7 #9 #11 13- I M7)

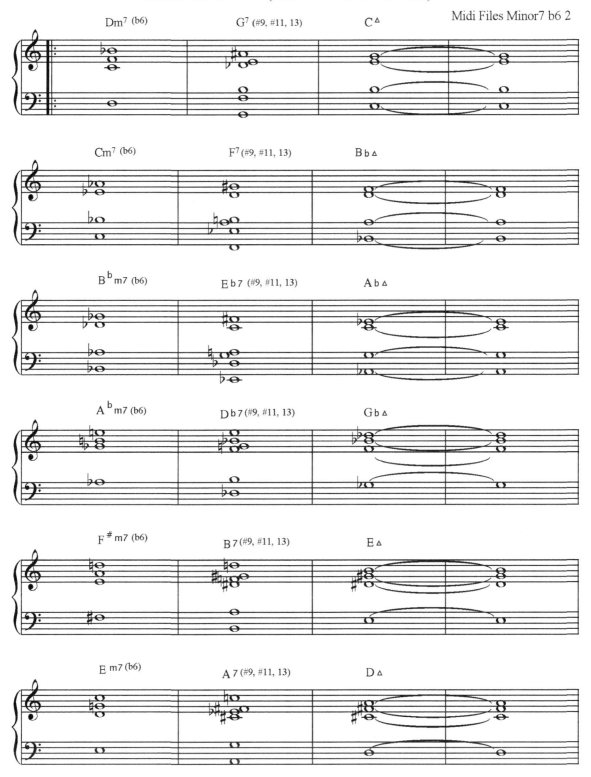

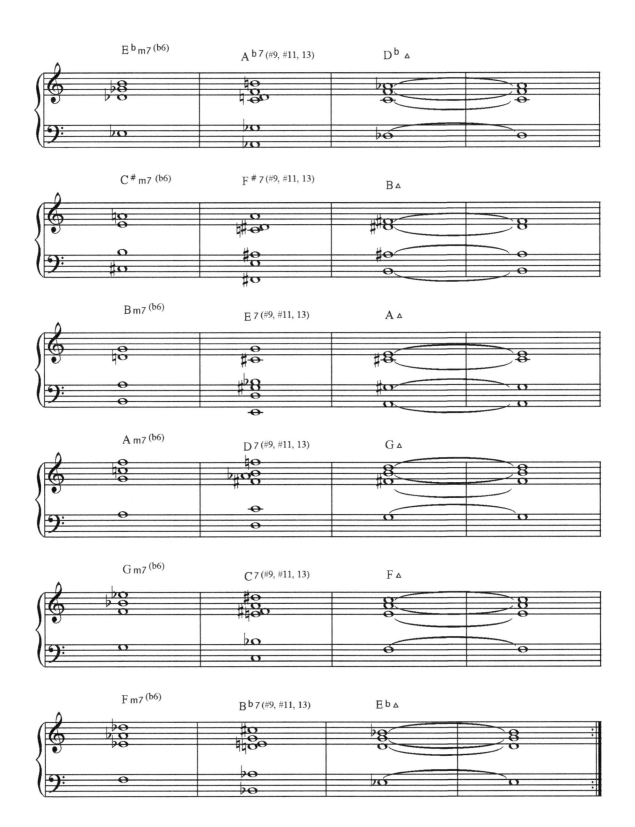

EXAMPLES OF ii-V-I (ii m7 b6- V Phrygian - I M7 9 #11 13)

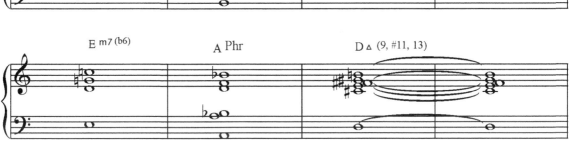

161

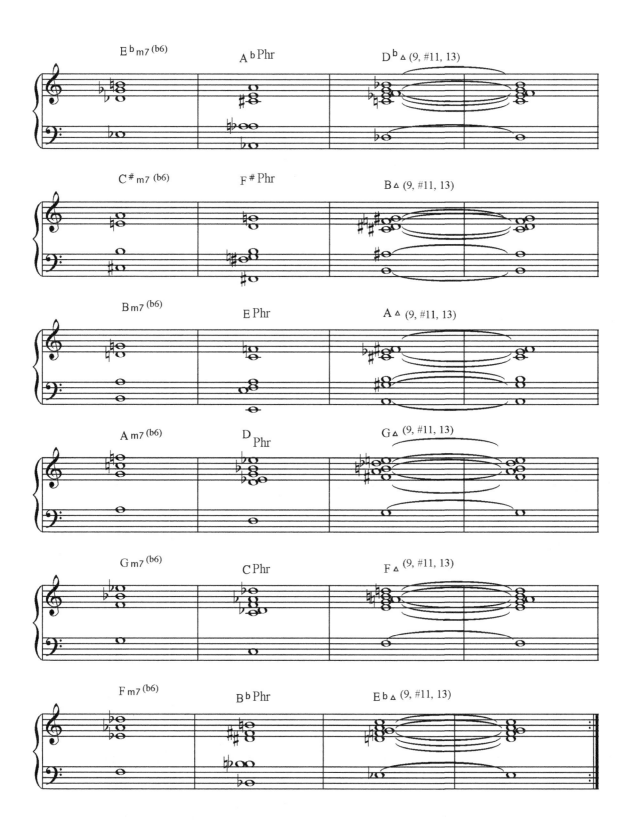

162

Slash Chords

- A **Slash Chord** is a triad over a root or bass note, it is useful to re-harmonize and create modern sounds.

- El **Acorde Slash** es una triada sobre una tónica o nota, este acorde es muy usado para rearmonizar y crear sonidos modernos.

Slash Chords Midi File 1

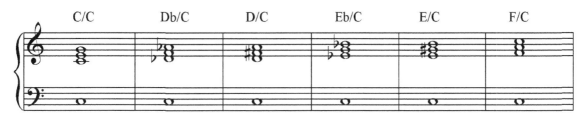

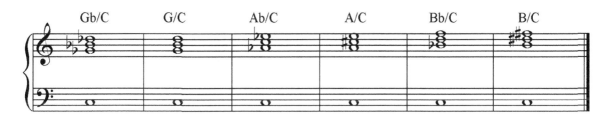

- ✓ Here we have some examples of Slash Chords/ Aquí tenemos unos ejemplos de los acordes Slash.

Slash Chords Midi Files 2

Slash Chord Reharmonization

Slash Chords Midi Files 3

EXAMPLES OF ii-V-I Slash Chords

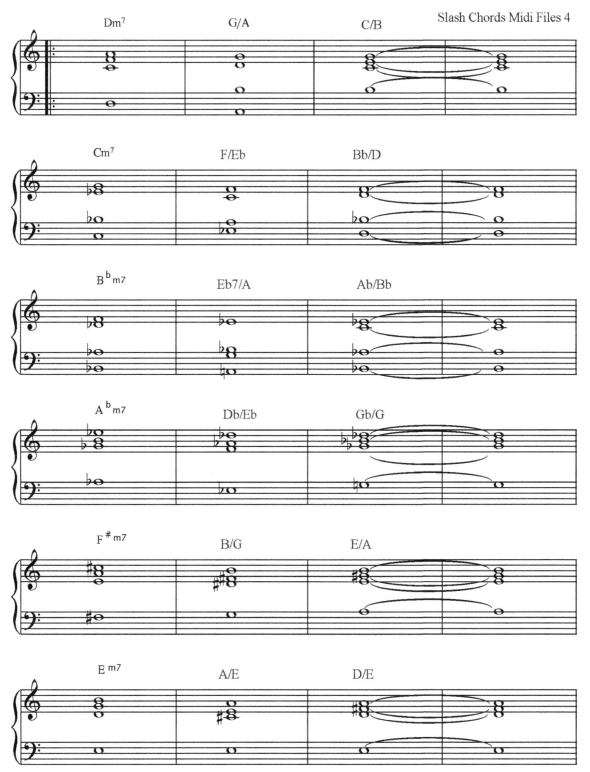

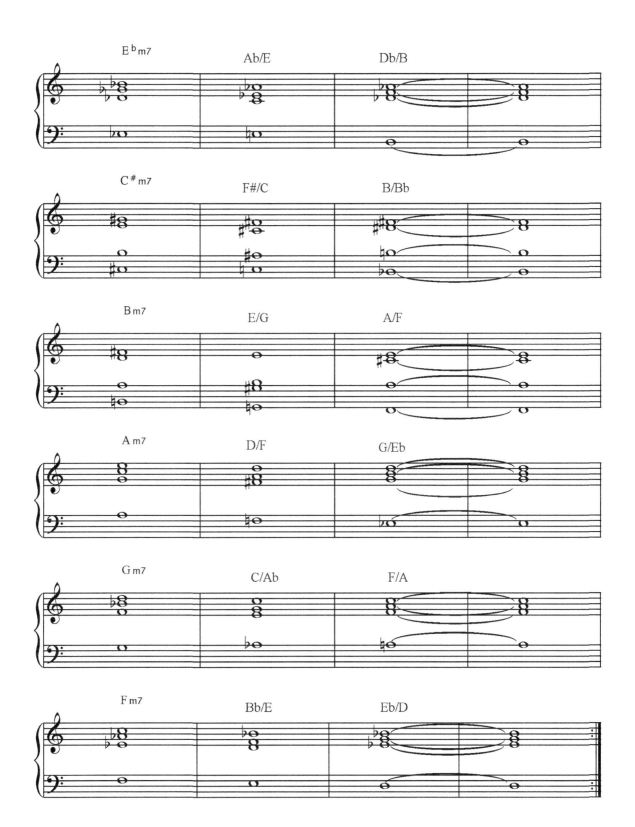

Drop 2

- A **Drop 2** is a technique that consists in dropping the second note from the top of the chord down an octave.

- El **Drop 2** es una técnica que consiste en bajar la segunda nota de la parte de arriba del acorde una octava abajo.

- ✓ In the next example we have CMaj 7 (9) chord/ En el siguiente ejemplo tenemos un acorde CMaj 7 (9).

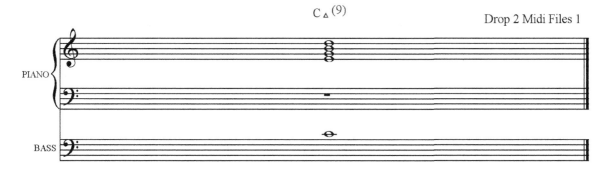

- ✓ Here is an example of how to apply Drop 2 technique on a Major7 (9) chord/ Aquí tenemos un ejemplo de cómo aplicar la técnica de Drop 2 en un acorde Mayor7 (9).

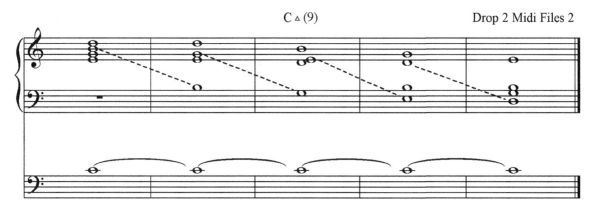

- ✓ I recommend to apply the Drop 2 technique in all Major7 (9, #11, 13) & Minor7 (9, 11, 13)/ Recomiendo aplicar esta técnica en los acorde Mayores (9, #11, 13) & Menores (9, 11, 13).

Tritone Substitution

- A **Tritone** is a musical interval composed by three whole tones. For example:

- El **Tritono** es un intervalo musical compuesto de tres tonos. Por ejemplo:

Tritone Substitution Midi File 1

Whole Note   Whole Note   Whole Note

- ✓ Here we have all the musical notes with its Tritone intervals/ Aquí tenemos todas las notas musicales con sus respectivos intervalos de Tritono.

Tritone Intervals   Tritone Substitution Midi Files 2

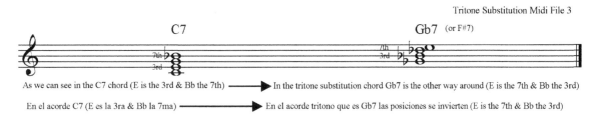

Tritone Substitution Chord

- ✓ A **Tritone substitution** chord is the substitution of one dominant 7th chord with another one sharing the most important elements of a chord the 3rd & 7th. For example:

- ✓ El **acorde tritono** remplaza a un acorde dominante lo que tienen en común es que comparten los elementos más importantes de un acorde que son la 3ra & 7ma. Por ejemplo:

Tritone Substitution Midi File 3

C7   Gb7 (or F#7)

As we can see in the C7 chord (E is the 3rd & Bb the 7th) ⟶ In the tritone substitution chord Gb7 is the other way around (E is the 7th & Bb the 3rd)

En el acorde C7 (E es la 3ra & Bb la 7ma) ⟶ En el acorde tritono que es Gb7 las posiciones se invierten (E is the 7th & Bb the 3rd)

- Next page examples of ii- Tritone Sub- I/ Siguiente tenemos ejemplos de ii-Tritone Sub-I.

EXAMPLES OF ii-Tritone Sub-I (i m7 9- TSub- I M7)

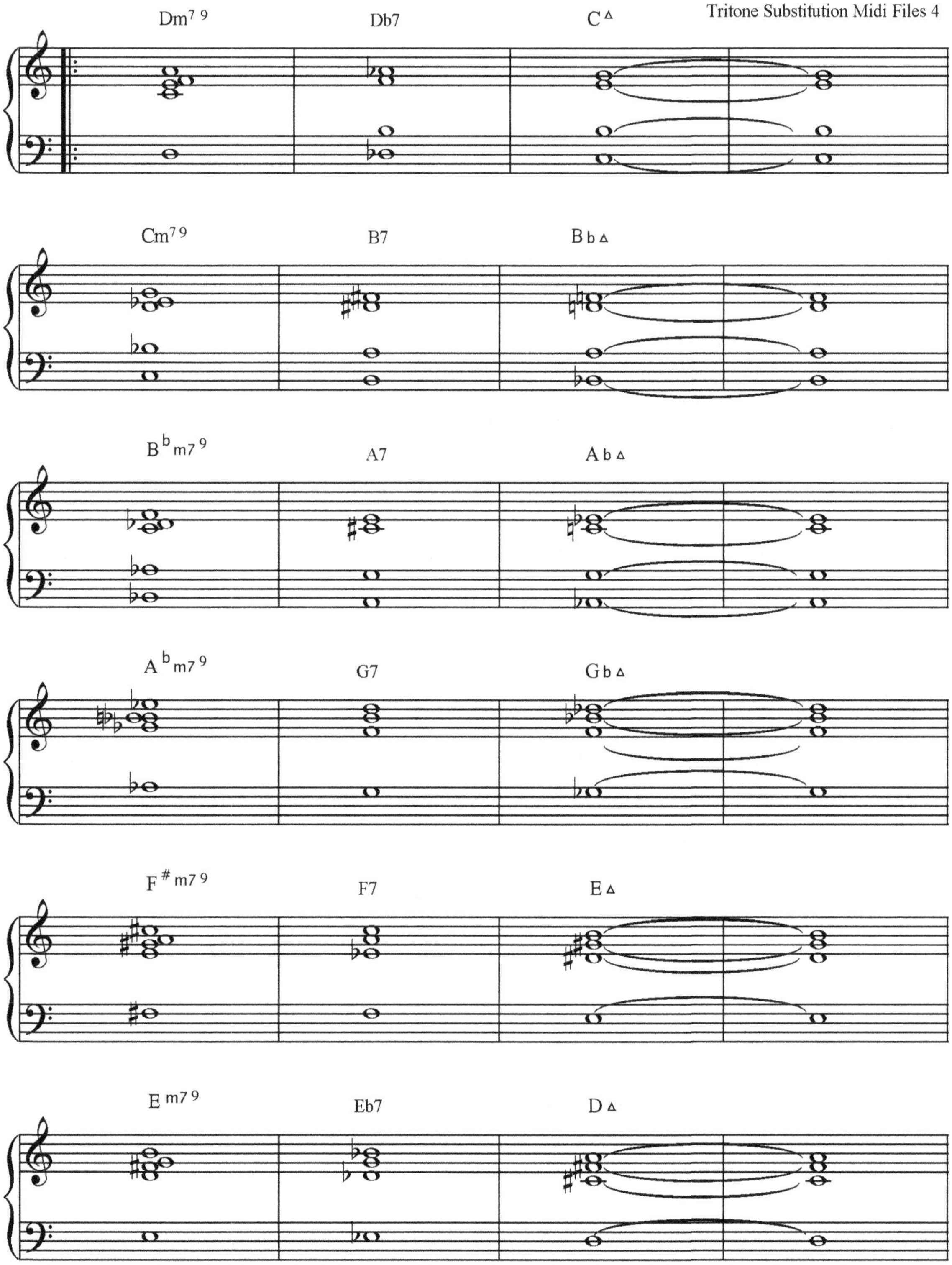

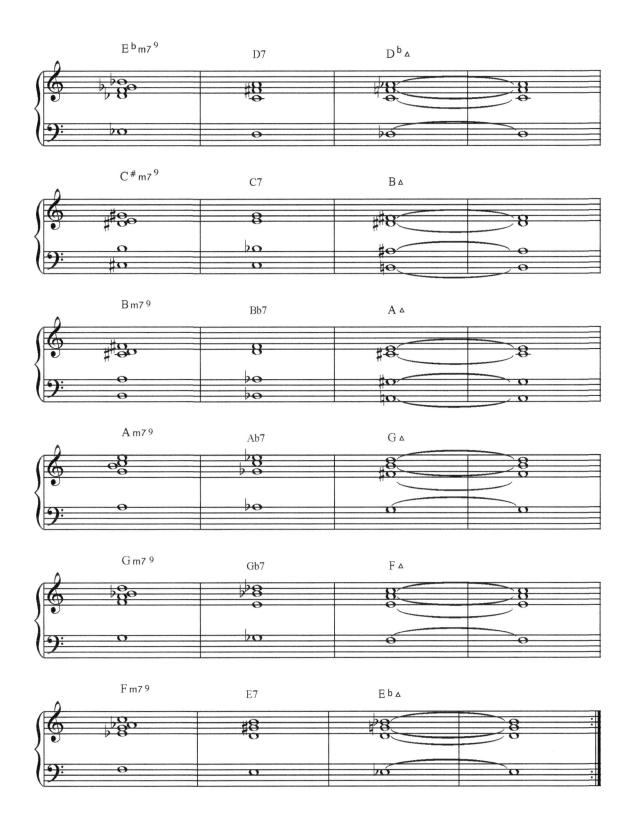

EXAMPLES OF ii-Tritone Sub with "Extentions"-I (i m7 9- TSub- I M7)

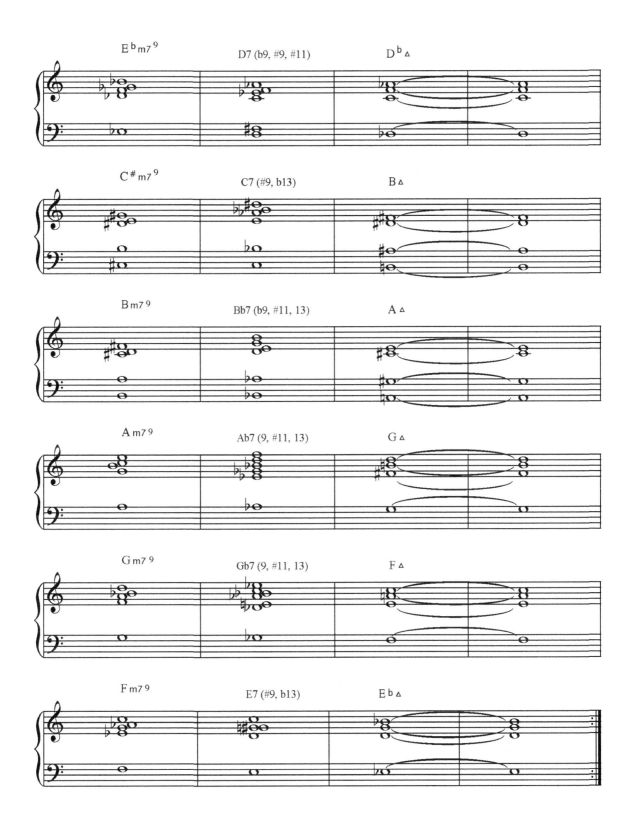

Pedal Point

- It is playing a sequence of chords over the same bass note.

- Es cuando tocamos una secuencia de acordes sobre una nota en el bajo.

✓ For Example/ Por Ejemplo:

Pedal Point Midi File 1

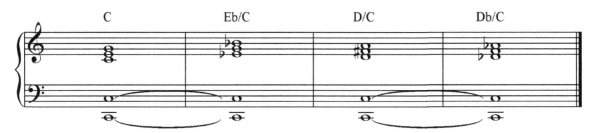

Pedal Point Midi File 2

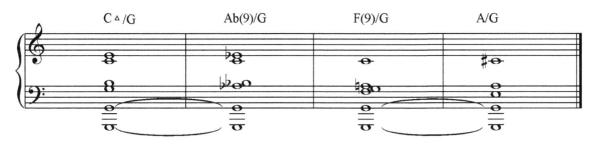

Pedal Point Midi File 3

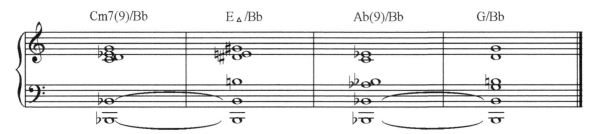

EXAMPLES OF ii-V-I (ii m7 9 11- V7 #9- I M7 / Pedal Point

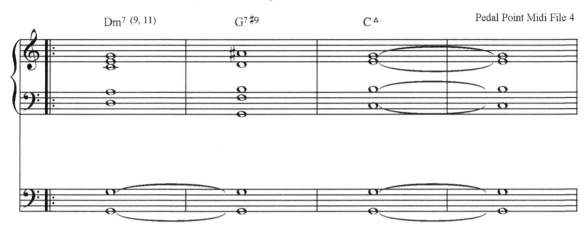

Dm⁷ ⁽⁹, ¹¹⁾   G⁷ #9   Cᐃ   Pedal Point Midi File 4

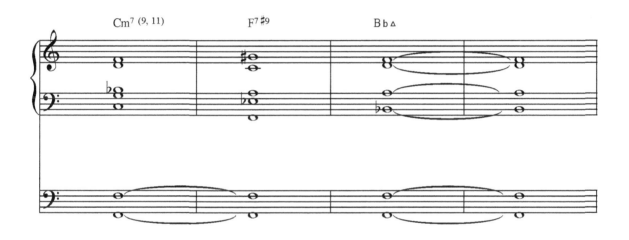

Cm⁷ ⁽⁹, ¹¹⁾   F⁷ #9   Bbᐃ

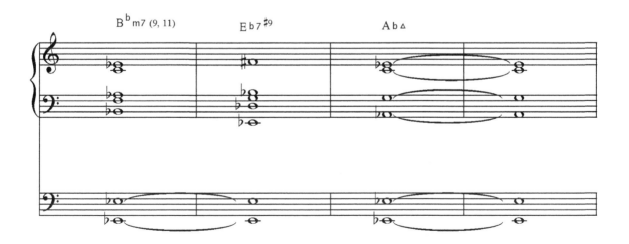

Bbm7 ⁽⁹, ¹¹⁾   Eb7 #9   Abᐃ

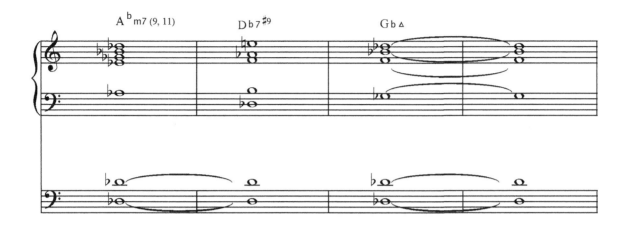

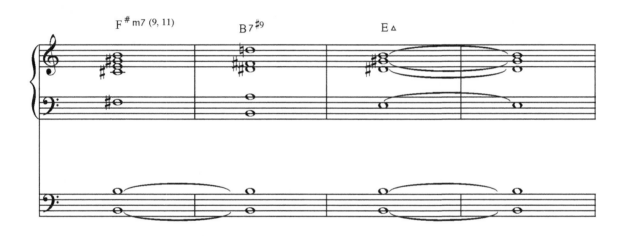

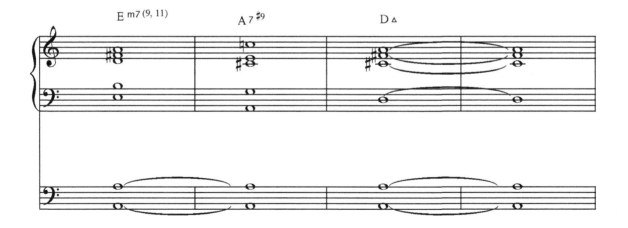

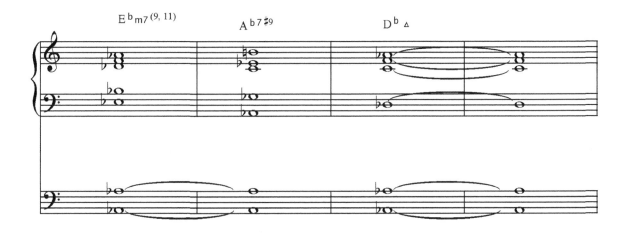

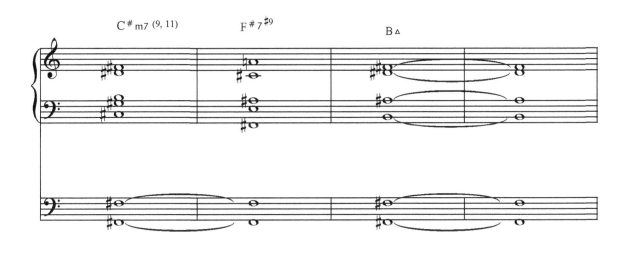

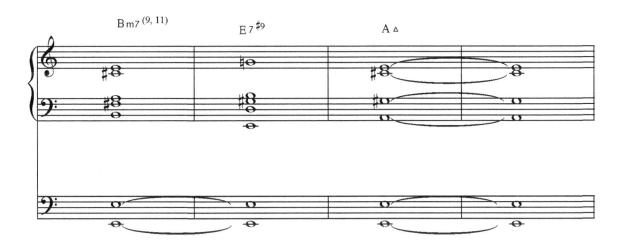

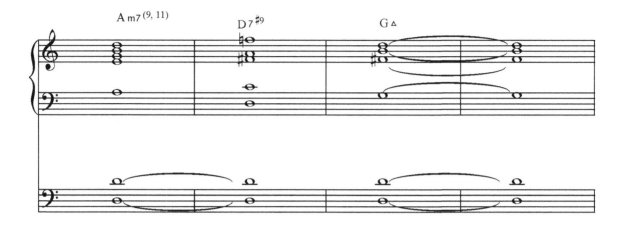

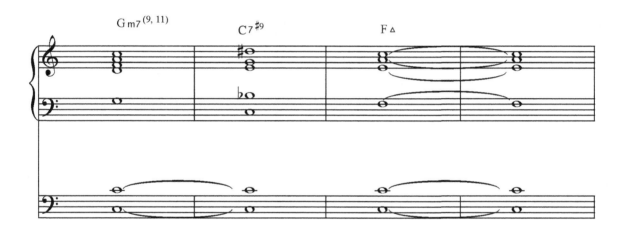

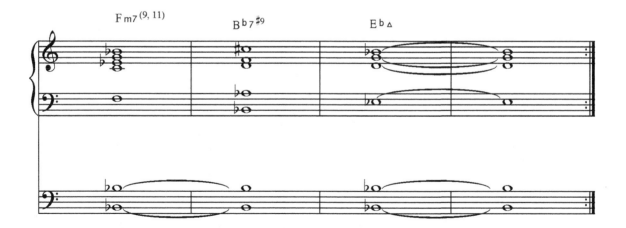

Melodic Minor Scale Harmony

- The **Melodic Minor** scale is a seven-note scale & has seven modes; its sound is dark and modern.

- La **Escala Melódica** menor está compuesta de siete notas & modos. Esta escala tiene un sonido muy oscuro y moderno.

Combination of Melodic Minor Chords (2-5-1)

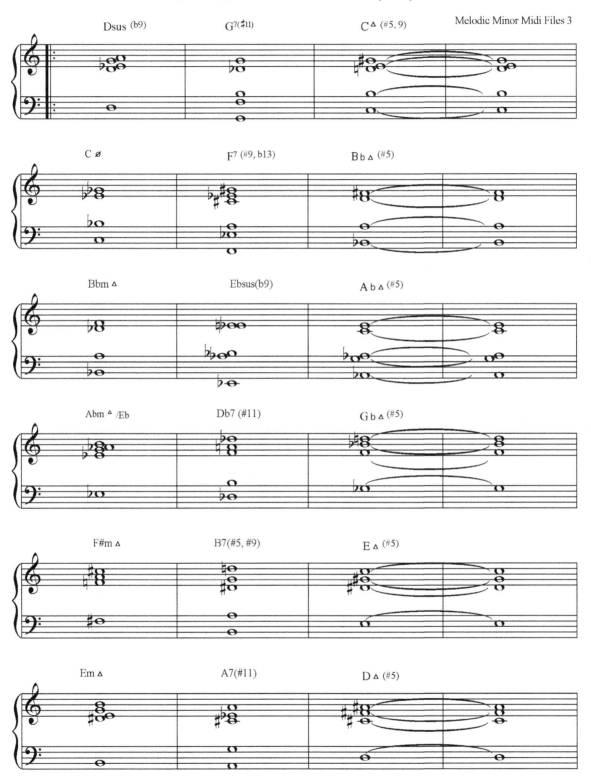

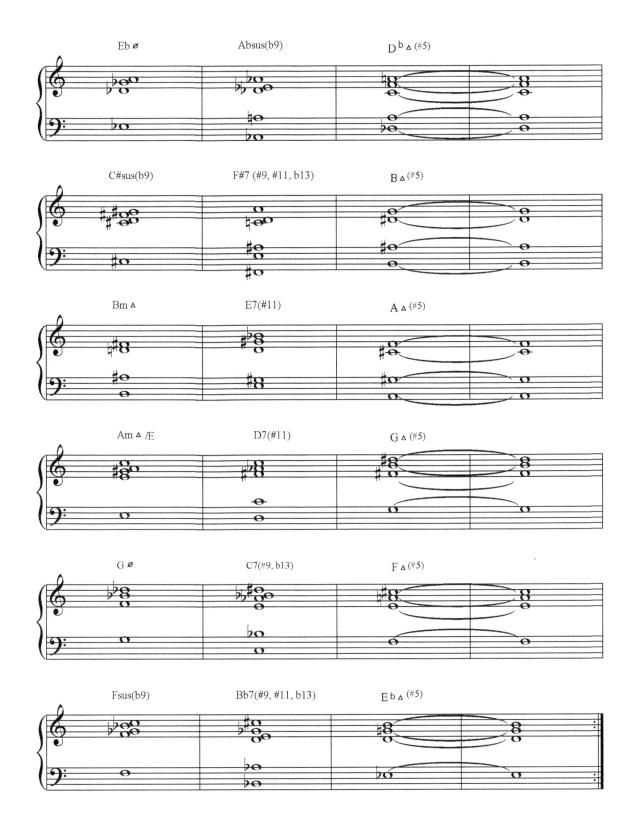

Working on this book has been an amazing journey. I encourage You to remember, "The future belongs to those who believe in the beauty of their dreams." *Eleanor Roosevelt*

Trabajar en este libro ha sido una experiencia Hermosa. Te recomiendo que siempre recuerdes que "El futuro le pertenece a aquellos que creen en la belleza de sus sueños." *Eleanor Roosevelt*

KIKI SANCHEZ

Credits/Créditos

Production Manager: Kiki Sanchez

Editor: Lynn Leon

Proof Reader: Kiki Sanchez

Art Director: Juan Carlos Flores Ruiz

Photo Editor: Juan Carlos Flores Ruiz

Kiki Sanchez is available Master Classes and Music Workshops; for more information contact us at:

Kiki Sanchez está disponible para Clases Maestras y Talleres; para más información contactar:

www.kikisanchez.com

Email: info@kikisanchez.com

Phone: (786) 505-6832